Men! What's missing in today's Church

Derek Cook has been researching the issue of why churches attract more women than men for over four years, and is particularly concerned about wives whose husbands do not share their Christian faith. As founder director of Maranatha Ministries, a Christian teaching centre, he and his wife Lilian run nationwide 'Missing Men' and 'Husbands and the Kingdom' seminars that cover the subject of this book.

Previously an employee of ICI, Derek is an ordained Baptist minister and is seconded as an evangelist by the Baptist Union and works with churches of all denominations.

He lives in Kirkby Stephen, Cumbria.

Acknowledgements

Any book has to be the product of a team of people and I am grateful to all those who have been part of the team over the last few years.

They deserve a word of thanks.

My wife Lilian has been involved in much of the research behind my writing. She has checked material and added many helpful insights in the early and later stages of production. I could not have done without her.

Other members of the Maranatha Team have also played a vital part. My thanks to Hazel for typing and typing, to Jennie for helping to run the Teaching Centre, and to John Irwin, Jon Cook and Malcolm Worsley for being both colleagues and friends.

My hideaway in Scotland, where most of the manuscript was written over a hectic four-week period, was with a doctor's delightful family in Bo'ness. It was great fun for me, staying with Tom and Elspeth, Brian and Moira; they just had to read Hebrews chapter thirteen verse two.

The book came into being because of the gentle persistence of Christine Whitell, Publishing Manager of Marshall Pickering. She has the spiritual gift of encouragement.

Derek Cook, September 1991

Men!
What's missing in today's Church

by
Derek Cook

MarshallPickering
An Imprint of HarperCollins*Publishers*

Marshall Pickering is an Imprint of
HarperCollins*Religious*
Part of HarperCollins*Publishers*
77–85 Fulham Palace Road, London W6 8JB

First published in Great Britain
in 1992 by Marshall Pickering

1 3 5 7 9 10 8 6 4 2

A catalogue record for this book is
available from the British Library

ISBN 0 551 02588-3

Typeset by Medcalf Type Ltd, Bicester, Oxon

Printed and bound in Great Britain by
HarperCollinsManufacturing Glasgow

Contents

Preface

The six-year-old son of the minister with whom I was staying was called in for lunch.

He was clearly upset that he hadn't been able to finish playing a game of football with his friends.

'Have you washed your hands?' asked his mother. It was obvious from the state of him that he hadn't.

'No!' came the reply. 'Well, go and wash them please. You know what I am always telling you about germs.'

The little lad shuffled off to the downstairs loo and as he went I heard him mutter, 'Germs and Jesus. Germs and Jesus. That's all I ever hear about in this house, and I've never seen either of them.'

That sounds about par for the course when it comes to the average man's attitude to Jesus Christ.

In this book I want to tell you how we can make the Christian message plain to modern men. I want to encourage, enable and challenge Church leaders to get on with this vital task.

If you happen to be a woman who has found personal faith in Christ which at the moment isn't shared by your partner, then I have something important to share with you. God hasn't given up on your man yet!

Read this book and you will be far better equipped to answer his questions and far more confident about what God can do.

I also hope that some of my readers will be men who are seeking for a personal faith for themselves. I have written honestly about the realities that I observe. I am also totally convinced that Jesus Christ is the GOD/MAN who deserves and demands your allegiance. I hope that through these pages He will find you.

Section One

The differences that exist

Chapter 1

The men our churches are missing

The churches in the United Kingdom are losing one hundred men every day. That is the stark, tragic fact revealed by the Marc Europe survey of churches published in 1991.

That means there has been an overall loss of over 360,000 men over the last ten years. An overall loss means that the men who are going home to glory are not being replaced in the ranks of the church. It also means that men who had been attending have stopped coming. It further implies that the husbands of wives who have become believers through church activities have been left out in the dark as far as real faith is concerned.

I do not think that church leaders have come to terms with the situation. Indeed in some circles the leaders that I have talked to do not appear to know that anything has changed. This is usually because they are so busy doing emergency work in their churches that they never do any careful surveys of where they have reached, nor an analysis of changes that are taking place under their noses.

Acknowledging the problem

To give just one example: we asked the leadership of a

church in the south of England if they had many wives in their church who had uncommitted partners. Their answer was an immediate, 'No, we don't have that problem.' On further questioning, they admitted that they might actually have one or two. A fortnight later after some more careful thought and research they came back to tell us that our observation was correct and that there were twenty-three women in this situation. Could we come and do some teaching that would help them? The teaching that needs to be done first of all, is to teach the church not to be so sexist in its activities. Over the last three years, we have checked out several hundred churches representing all the denominations and strands within the church today. All of them were running at least one activity for women. A young wives' group, a sisterhood meeting, a Bible study for ladies, aerobics, mums and toddlers; the list is endless. Most churches were running several activities for women.

Many women had come to real faith because of the friendships first built up with Christian women through one or another of those activities. I am thrilled that this work of God is going on and want it to reach more and more women for the Kingdom. Tragically, however, of all the churches reaching out to women only 30 per cent had any bridge-building activity for men.

The women were catered for with activities that they could attend, often outside the church premises and dealing with real and relevant issues. The men, on the other hand, were treated as second class citizens. Their only invitation was to come along to a Sunday service. That seems to me to be totally unfair treatment.

One minister in Birmingham said that he wouldn't run any informal activity just for men because, 'that would be sexist.' But surely his women's meeting and young wives' groups are sexist? You can't have it one way only.

Did you know, incidentally, that most ladies' toilets in churches have mirrors but that many of the men's toilets have no mirror? Is this why men don't attend as often, because they cannot comb their hair and make an impression on everyone else? Every man knows that, 'You never get a second chance to make a first impression.'

First impressions

So what is the first impression any man gets who does attend your church? Do you only present notices which advertise events for women? Are the posters on display those lovely, pretty ones, the ones with animals and children? All these serve to suggest that church is for women and children

Is there broken furniture and other out of date items lying around? That could prove that no men attend because a man good with his hands would have sorted out this lot a long time ago.

We just don't realise the visual impact that our churches have upon men. I haven't even mentioned the chairs – but I'm going to! Has your church got any? In the worship area, I mean. Victorian pews were made for Victorian people just as King James English was understood by King James's subjects.

The pews of the 1890s were comfortable for the smaller men of those days. My researchers tell me that they were not so comfortable for the women of that era. Nowadays, because everyone is better fed and taller than they used to be, the pews are more or less right for the women of the 1990s but very uncomfortable for the men of today. Next time you see that visiting, uncommitted husband squirming in his seat, remember that it might not be the conviction of the Holy Spirit getting through to him; it might be that you have gone on for far too long, and he is sitting down whereas you are standing up.

To return to those devastating Marc Europe statistics. In 1979 the percentage of male churchgoers was 45 per cent to the female 55 per cent. By 1989 the percentage of male attenders had fallen to 42 per cent against the female 58 per cent. There is evidence to suggest that as the proportion of women in a church increases, so it becomes more difficult for the uncommitted man to start attending that church. On present trends alone, we will soon be in the position where two-thirds of the congregation in the average church will be women. Setting that against the population statistics which show that in the total population only 51 per cent are women and 49 per cent are men, and adding the fact that in the younger age groups men now outnumber women, you can see what a failure we have become. And things are only set to get worse unless we do something now.

A church at war

So who can we blame? Well, it is true to say that some of the losses can be traced back to the Great War of 1914–18. You only have to look at the memorials in older churches to see how a generation of men were taken out at that time. In particular a whole group of creatively thinking men were taken from the church.

During those war years the women took over the tasks that their husbands had relinquished when they went off to war. The loyalty of these women to their menfolk meant that they kept the church as it was. They expected their husbands to be home soon and wanted everything to be unchanged when the men came home. As a result, much of church life between the wars became a pattern of economising and maintaining things as they had always been.

May I remind you that the church is still at war. Our enemy has been on the move and has been snatching away men. C S Lewis suggests that the Devil sustains himself by feeding on men.

I am passionately concerned to change the situation and revolutionise the church in its ability to reach men with the good news of what life can become through Jesus and the power of God, the Holy Spirit.

I am campaigning to see creativity in evangelism when it comes to reaching out to men. Risk-taking certainly appears to appeal to younger men. There is clear evidence that churches which have embarked upon new building, or imaginative re-building projects, have succeeded in attracting more men as a result. Men want to be associated with success. Let's tell them the greatest success story of all time, namely how the GOD/MAN rose from the dead, and how we can do the same, living forever in His eternal Kingdom.

I am also concerned for the new breed of professional women managers. The church is failing to present the Gospel to them as well. Indeed many churches do not even seem to know that such a significant group of thoughtful people exists.

Are all our present evangelistic activities merely storing up problems for the future of our churches? Six years ago a church told me that they were about to start a new outreach programme by opening a mum's and toddler's facility at their church. I suggested that they should think again. I saw the need for the work that they planned but I wanted them to think through the long term effects. Wives would come along. They would meet attractive Christian women. They would begin to ask questions about the faith that they saw in these folk. The church would pray for such interested people. They would hear and would believe.

What about their husbands? I asked. What opportunities are you going to set up for them? What practical advice will you offer about being a father in today's world? How do they handle the discipline of their children? What implications are there if the woman becomes a believer? How does this affect the issue of headship in the home? Can you think out some ways to treat the couples as couples? Can you make the faith exciting for them together?

I was not trying to dampen down the enthusiasm to reach the young wives but I was asking for some thought to be given, from the start of the project, to the men who would also be involved.

Sadly, they misunderstood what I was trying to say. They thought that I was against setting up mum's and toddler's groups. They have just written to me again. My predictions and projections have all come true. Women have been converted but the husbands have not been reached at all. There is tension over faith in several homes. One man has walked out on his wife saying bitterly, 'You are not the woman I married.' One wife was on the receiving end of violence when she returned from the midweek meeting recently. The church has run itself aground on a whole series of marital rocks because it didn't chart its course before it left the harbour.

Unreachable?

'But nothing can be done to reach men; they won't come to our family services,' said another group of church leaders to me. I had to admit that this church was right. I don't think that I would have gone either except for the fact that I had a job to do there. Very often the preaching at a family service is geared for the younger children, so the men get the message that our Christianity is juvenile. I have seen some men blackmailed into attending a family service. 'The children are taking part so you will come, darling.' Of course, he can't refuse.

When he gets to church there are more women and children present than usual. So you reinforce his idea that church is for the women and children. Then, for the man, there are so many distractions. Children moving, being noisy. The women take it all in their stride. They are not distracted by the noise of children. The only time that a woman becomes concerned is if her little one suddenly goes quiet – that must mean that he is up to some mischief.

But amid all the noise, the man is totally distracted. Now please don't misunderstand me. I am not against family services, but I am saying that they are probably not the best first event, to use to try and bring a man into contact with the church. Most family services are really children's services.

Men can be reached. But they don't usually respond to activities which ask them to admit their needs. Men spend most of their lives covering up any vulnerable spots. What do you think Adam wanted his figleaf for?

You will find, however, that men are into discovery. They do have ideals, dreams and aspirations. Run an informal group on discovering the best way to invest money and you will meet the aspirations of many men who are trying to plan for the future of their families. Plan an evening on how to make credit cards work for you and you will reach those struggling to make financial ends meet. Run a discussion event on lessons that men have learnt on how to bring up children. How much pocket money at what age? How late can a youngster stay out? Who tells them about sex and how do you tell them? The men will come to real events to share their success stories and end by sharing their failures as well. And in the midst of it all, some can share their faith.

Notice that I try to avoid the use of the word 'meeting'. Please don't invite men along to meetings. He has enough of meetings at work. Most meetings are a waste of time or a time of conflict. He doesn't want any more in the evenings, thank you very much.

Bright ideas

Here is a church just north of London. They have started a Saturday breakfast for men. It is held about every six weeks. The dates are fixed by the availability of the right kind of speaker. Uncommitted men have been glad to accept the invitation to attend. The treat of a cooked breakfast, followed by an ex-SAS man telling about the excitement of being a follower of Jesus Christ, proved irresistible. Now the outsider men are bringing their non-Christian friends.

In another part of the country there is a business man who has recently become a Christian, taking the initiative because his church wasn't doing anything to reach men. He invited a Christian golf professional to give a demonstration and some coaching at his own club. Then they played a round. Fourteen men came along, only four of them believers. At the end, over drinks, all four of them were asked by the others to say how they had come to faith. Where did the money came from to stage such an event? The new Christian simply used his tithe. Now I have to say that some of the church leaders were not happy that he used his money in that way. They felt that the church finance should be his major commitment. His answer was simple: 'You do the evangelism job of the church, and my money will go into your collection plate.'

The churches in the United Kingdom are losing men at an overall rate of one hundred a day. Together, you and I are going to change that statistic.

Let's think for a moment about all the men with whom we are already in contact. In particular, I have a great concern for those wives who have come to personal faith and as yet their husbands do not share that faith. My conservative estimate is that the number in the United Kingdom comes somewhere near 500,000.

If every church in the country were to win just one man for Christ this year as a result of the challenge of this book, then we would see at least 48,000 more men in the Kingdom of God within a year. Join me in making that a realistic prayer target.

Let's start with the husbands that we already know about. Perhaps you'd like to discuss some of the possibilities.

Action page

For leaders or for group discussion. Maybe just the men should take a look at these questions together.

How many weekly activities do we run in our church for women?

How many activities of any kind are geared for men?

Let's do some creative thinking on this matter. How about some crazy ideas?

How many Christian wives with uncommitted husbands do we know about? (Don't be vague. Compile a list of the men's names for prayer.)

Who are the evangelists in our church?

Can we release some men from routine church duties to concentrate on reaching men for Christ?

Chapter 2

Is anyone to blame?

I want to say one thing very clearly and categorically to any women who have become Christian believers but whose partners do not, at this moment in time, share their Christian faith.

You are not to blame because your husband is not yet a believer.

The Devil's tactic is a very simple one. He wants you to feel guilty that your partner has not yet come to faith. The old enemy says something like, 'If you had prayed for him more, he would be a believer by now.' Or he suggests that, 'The reason he isn't a Christian is because you haven't talked to him enough about the Christian faith.' Oh yes, the Devil is quite capable of saying anything that will make you feel that it is 'all your fault.' The Devil aims to discourage the children of God. He has already lost you; he doesn't want to lose your partner to the Kingdom of light as well. So the evil one aims to make you feel gloomy, despairing, discouraged. If he can manage that, then you won't be a very good advert for radiant Christianity, will you?

Your gloom and discouragement will make your husband say, 'I've got enough problems at work without adding this

Christianity thing!' Discouraged Christian wives are not good adverts for the faith. Whatever you have tried, the Devil will tell you that you did it wrong. 'Your husband isn't yet a believer', says the old enemy, 'because you haven't invited him to enough things at church.' Alternatively he may say, 'It's because you've invited him to too many things at church.' Or, 'You've not talked to him enough,' or, 'You've talked to him too much.' Even, 'You haven't believed for him.' Whatever you have done, the Devil will tell you that you have done it wrong.

I want to tell you quite straightforwardly that it is not 'all your fault' that your partner is still uncommitted.

My research shows that the church has let you down.

How can we help?

In a survey conducted by Maranatha Ministries, I asked wives, 'Are there any other ways in which Christians could help you more?'

Here are some of the answers:

'I wish there were some informal meetings at the church I attend, to which I could bring my husband for discussion.'

'By treating us as a family, I feel like a single mum.'

'Activities run by Christian men for men. Our church focuses on the youth and therefore does not have the resources for men's groups.'

'Invites to purely social events with no sting in the tail.'

'If only Christian men would invite him to something.'

Let me spell it out again for believing wives whose partners are not yet in the Kingdom – it is not all your fault; the church has let you down.

I have a theory about men in the church today. I am beginning to think that some church leaders feel threatened if there are too many men around. The simple reason is that men tend to challenge things. They question the way things are done. They evaluate the effectiveness of some activities and ask why we still bother to run them at all. Women, by and large, accept things as they are. If a church changes to a new hymn book the women will learn the new songs and co-operate. Men, especially mature men who become followers of Christ, tend to challenge much more. They want to know why the church doesn't have all its songs on overhead projector. If the screen is too small to be seen at the back of the church then, 'Why on earth don't you buy a bigger screen?'

Men tend to be much more awkward to handle in church congregation discussion meetings. 'Can we have this information?' they ask. One recently converted businessman got up to ask about the church's main task. 'Is it really all about presenting the message of Jesus to those who are outside the church?' He was assured that, as an evangelical church, that was the real purpose for their existence. 'Then why, please,' he asked, 'do we only spend six per cent of our annual budget on evangelism and overseas mission and ninety four per cent on ourselves?' Good question. But not one which the leaders wanted to have pointed out to them.

I had this lovely experience in a parish church once. The vicar was in the middle of his sermon. He used what is called a rhetorical question. That is, he asked a question which he didn't intend anyone to answer; he was planning to give his own answer. 'Do you know what it's like out there in the real world outside our church?' he asked. He had waved his hand dramatically towards the windows looking out onto the housing estate. He paused for effect, and a man in the front row who had only been a Christian for about three weeks got up and told the vicar just what it was really like out there in the real world. You could tell he was a new Christian because he still thought that the best seats at any show were down at the front. As well as that, no one had told him that you don't interrupt the vicar in the middle of one of his sermons.

Training for the ministry

I want to ask all our theological training colleges to look again at their training of men for the ministry. Why are so many church leaders threatened by the presence of other men in their churches? Can you train men who are so confident about their own call that they can use every man in the church to be a part of the team which gets the work done? Can you instil into your pastoral training the fact that the husbands are a vital part of the family; concentrating on the women and children is not enough.

The church, and especially its leadership, has to take the responsibility for the weak and ineffectual presentation of Christianity to men. Often, in ministerial training college, the art of evangelism has been neglected. Pastoralia is all about caring for mums after childbirth or widows after bereavement. Ministers are trained to be those who bind up the broken hearted. It is conveniently forgotten that Jesus didn't include those words when he quoted from Isaiah 61. Jesus spoke about anointing and freedom, release and proclamation.

Ministerial students come out of college having been taught to be shepherds and then are sent to the inner cities where the sheep don't exactly grow on trees. A whole generation of ministers were taught to be servants of the church. It is true that Jesus chose to wash feet. But he rejected Peter's 'demand' to wash all of him. In other words Jesus was always in charge, even in the servanthood role.

Peacemakers and politicians have been seen as necessary,

but aggressive searching for the men who have wandered away has not been taught as an option.

Not many ministers play for the local football team or referee in the league. Not many ministers set aside time to be members of some man's activity in town. It is expected of the minister that he will play the role of priest to the women and children of the parish.

Ministers may feel unconsciously threatened by new men from outside the church. Within the church, too, the leadership often doesn't want any competition either. Most leaders have risen from the ranks after years of apprenticeship. Sometimes they represent the church as it once used to be, rather than in its present format.

Here is a Baptist church in an area where new housing development has replaced a factory site and where many of the terraces have become *pied-à-terre*, upmarket and modernised. A significant number of young couples have joined the church having moved from other towns and areas. The attractive young minister and his even more attractive wife have two little children of their own.

His leadership team – the Baptists call them deacons – consists of five elderly men and one retired headmistress. They feel under siege by all these new people. They have to keep dealing with requests for change. If they are not careful there will soon be more of these outsiders than members of the original congregation. There may even be a challenge for places on the diaconate. They say, 'Thank God for that church rule which says that people must have been members of the church for five years before they can stand for election to any church office.' That has made sure that the brilliant young musician who has just arrived cannot replace dear old tone-deaf Miss Bindley on the organ.

I exaggerate just a little to make the point but my travels throughout the United Kingdom have taken me to far too many churches where the above is hardly any exaggeration at all.

I have come to the conclusion that in the task of winning men for the Kingdom of God the biggest single hindrance is the church itself.

Resisting change

Dr R M Kanter in her book *The Change Masters*, produced a valuable study on leading world companies.

She talked to the senior managers and policy makers and looked at the structures of companies which had been successful but which were now beginning to struggle. She makes three telling observations.

As men rise in a company so they become increasingly isolated from the real world outside their company.

Then they become cut off from criticism.

Then they grow suspicious of ideas from those lower down the structure.

She was talking about the business world but it is an accurate description of the leadership in most of the churches that I have ever visited. Ministers and church officials are chosen or elected because they know how things should be in the church. The problem is that they have often forgotten how things are in the world. Surrounded in the church by older ladies or, if the church is more successful, by young mums and toddlers, these leaders cater for what they have got. This ensures that men will be increasingly isolated and alienated.

If, by a miracle of grace, a new man comes to know the Lord, the leadership will resent his challenge to their way of doing things and form a committee to look at his suggestions. Then in the worst of church traditions the committee never files its report. I even know of one case where the young man brought a prophetic word to the church. He was too new a Christian to know that it was a God-given gift of prophecy. The leaders' reaction was to ask him nicely if he would find himself another church to attend.

Of course, our churches dare not say that they don't want any new men, but as the Rev Eddie Gibbs once wryly observed. 'They practise discreet, spiritual birth control.'

The task of winning men must be seen as the priority for the Decade of Evangelism in the 1990s.

Lifeboat churches

Lifeboat churches – women and children first – have spelled out a clear message that men are not wanted. The impression has been given to a whole generation of men that Christianity is not for them.

'I love my husband', wrote one woman, 'and I love God, and it makes me so unhappy that the two whom I love most are not even on speaking terms.'

Wives speak of not being able to share any more the discoveries and thrill of their Christian faith with a husband who is beginning to tell her that she has gone over the top with all this religious stuff.

Wives vary in whether they try to drag their husband along to every church event in the hope that something will get through, to the other extreme of doing and saying nothing in the hope that what she had discovered will dawn on him. Unfortunately she had not taken into account her feminine bias towards the spiritual dimension of life and her husband's built-in mind set which makes him slower and thicker when it comes to the issues of the spirit.

The trouble with dragging him off to everything is that it can become really difficult. There are the children to take along as well. That probably means that the event will have a family bias. All he sees are lots of women and children. The few Christian men are probably in the deacon's vestry having a prayer time. (By the way, how is the visiting man supposed to know that? All he sees are this group of smiling men coming out from a side room. Perhaps they have been having a smoke or a drink together. And what does he think if they all have long faces?)

I have to say that if you are trying to win your husband by praying him along to church events, then you need to be very selective indeed about what you take him along to. The event needs to have a period when the Christian message is explained in realistic, historical and jargon-free terms following a logical pattern and ending with an opportunity to make a personal, but not embarrassing, response. The speaker must have the gift of the evangelist, an evangelist being someone who can present the facts about Jesus Christ in such a way that makes a response possible.

A church that I heard about recently had organised an evening meal at a local restaurant and invited couples to be their guests. They approached a number of the unconverted husbands and invited them to bring their Christian wives. That is always the right way round, the invitation must go to the man. He has the chance to accept without feeling in competition with his wife. The restaurant setting was good. The meal was reasonable. The after dinner speaker brought along by the church was well known in church circles. He spoke about 'An apocalyptical comparative analysis between Daniel's time and times and half a time, and the revelation of John on Patmos.' You think I'm joking; sadly it is all true. You must forgive me that I feel angry at how the church had let down those Christian wives.

The speaker may have been a brilliant Bible teacher but he was not an evangelist. Those husbands needed to be exposed to a witty after dinner speaker whose anecdotes and personal experiences would have touched their minds and hearts. The men needed to be taken one step along the road to faith and given an opportunity to talk to another man or raise questions on a one to one basis afterwards. Some husbands needed follow through with a book to read or a video to take home to watch.

Why do some churches feel that humour is unspiritual? Why are some churches so behind the times that they haven't produced any material on video to loan to these fringe men? It was not the wife's fault that her husband came to the conclusion that Christianity was a lot of mumbo-jumbo.

Relevant strategies

Another danger arises when a husband is taken to hear a man with a famous testimony. He can easily come to the conclusion that faith is certainly needed by someone who fell out of an aeroplane at 2,000 feet without a parachute but who survived because a St Bernard dog dug him out of the snow drift that he landed in, but that such a faith is a remote factor for his own life in suburban Worcester.

I am not suggesting that such testimonies should be banned. They can appeal to some men, especially if they have just faced a crisis time themselves. Always aim to include in a testimony, however, a strong statement about the reality of Christ for today's events and ordinary lives.

Why not buy sufficient copies of a good evangelistic book

about Christianity and give one to every man who is in any way, however loosely, associated with your church? Then maybe some discussion groups in homes about a month later to talk about one particular chapter. The chapter to choose is the one which speaks of men taking the lead in guiding their families to God.

Or give a copy of my minibook *Help! My Wife's got Religion*, to every uncommitted husband whose wife attends your church. Don't ask the wife to give it to him – some may be able to but still shouldn't be asked. Send your Christian men out man to man. What my American friends call 'nose to nose.'

Then hold a meeting in a home to talk about it. Aim at a fifty/fifty mix of Christians and visitors. Let the husbands tear the book to pieces if they want. Let them ask all their awkward questions. Admit sometimes that you don't know all the answers. Be frank about the failures and mistakes that have been made, but tell them about the magnificent Jesus that you follow. At least one of them will get converted and he will become the means of winning some of the others. Churches that have tried it have found that it works.

Churches should seriously consider appointing a new full time staff member whose sole responsibility is reaching and winning men. Don't tell me that there wouldn't be enough work for him to do. He would need to be energetic and creative but his week wouldn't be long enough to contain all the opportunities.

Jesus said quite distinctly,

But I, when I am lifted up from the earth, will draw all men to myself (John 12:32).

Now is the time to lift Jesus higher in our churches and fellowships.

It's not all your fault!

Wives, it's not all your fault that your partner is not yet a believer. Stop blaming yourself and start enjoying your own walk with God. Don't give up hope about your husband coming to faith; there is still time. Where there is life there is hope. That's an old saying but it is true. Can you remember who was the first man ever to enter heaven? Yes, you've got it. It was the dying thief. Some friends of mine did a dramatic presentation of that occasion. The first man is due in heaven. The angels put out the gold and silver streamers. There is a fanfare of trumpets to welcome him. All the junior angels are lined up with flags to wave and told to cheer when he comes into sight. Two senior angels are there to shake his hand. And who turns up? A scruffy thief!

'Cor,' he says, 'I would 'ave nicked this lot a munf ago.' He must have come to the wrong place. The angels check his credentials. He has an invite from the Prince of Life Himself!

When did that man put his trust in Jesus Christ? Only a matter of minutes, or at most hours, before the end of his time on earth.

Never give up hope. Keep on praying for your husband and ask others in your church to pray for him by name. Tell us his name. Don't let us get away without knowing something about your husband. Even if he doesn't come to church, don't leave him as a shadowy figure in the background. Tell us something about him and then, if I telephone your home to ask for your help with a project and he answers, I can chat a little to him instead of just having to say, 'Is Jennie at home?'

Wives, of course, are not always perfect. In their eagerness for their husbands to share their Christian faith they do make mistakes. But God is not limited by our mistakes. If there have been some mistakes, learn from them. Commit everything to God. When sins have been confessed they are forgiven. Don't let the old enemy keep dragging them up again and again. The Devil is only out to dishearten and to depress you.

Praise God that more and more churches are waking up to the task of reaching men. Church leaders are already reading this book and some have begun to try out the ideas listed in the middle section of the book.

Chapter 3

A partnership in faith

Did you ever hear the apocryphal story about the nervous young bride? She was sure that she would totally forget what to do when she got to church, because she would be so excited.

Her minister came up with a marvellous solution. 'Look,' he said, 'I'll meet you and your father at the door. I'll make sure that you are on the right side of your father so that you'll be next to the bridegroom when you reach the front. All that you have to remember is to walk down the aisle to the front altar. Then I'll announce the opening hymn. By the time that you've sung your favourite hymn you will have calmed down, and it will all go ever so smoothly.'

On the day, she was radiant. Perfectly on time, beautiful in a marvellous dress. On the arm of her proud father she walked carefully down to the front of the church where Peter and the vicar were now waiting and with every step she repeated to herself, 'Aisle, Altar, Hymn.' 'Aisle, Altar, Hymn.' Of course she never did!

It is an old day-dream to feel that those minor irritations which we put up with during courtship will be removed miraculously by the wedding vows.

If she was always losing her car keys in the early days,

then the wedding ceremony is not likely to suddenly affect her memory in that department. Make sure you know where the keys are for the honeymoon trip.

He is also still likely to leave the top off the toothpaste seventeen years later, just as he did on the honeymoon. We all harbour ideas that we will be able to change our partner but they are not realistic hopes and the sooner we come to terms with that fact then the sooner we will get on with the task of adjusting and living in harmony with one another.

The first flush

In most relationships the early days include a number of emotional fireworks, usually unexpected. 'How did you know that this man was different?' I asked my friend Marion. 'Because every time he spoke to me, the hairs on the back of my neck stood on end,' was her reply.

That first kiss can be dynamite. It can take you by surprise. Sweep you off your feet. Do things to your equilibrium. It is the first flush of romance and it's great.

We have to face the fact that the romantic turn on of those early days rarely lasts for any length of time. If a couple have married quickly because of the buzz they gave to one another, then they may sadly part when the buzz becomes a drone. Modern divorce arrangements make it all too easy for them to slip out of commitment as quickly as they went in.

But the romance part is only for starters. The main course is much heavier and much better for you. It involves working at loving one another. So the early foothills of romance need to grow into the mountains of trust and mutual respect.

For couples who stay together, later years may lack some

of the fireworks of romance but they include many more frequent times of multicoloured contentment.

Lawrence Crabb in his book *Marriage Builder* puts it this way:

Husbands and wives are to regard marriage as an opportunity to minister in a unique and special way to another human being, to be used of God to bring their spouses into a more satisfying appreciation of their worth as persons who are secure and significant in Jesus Christ.

Such realism involves giving one another room to grow up as people. The person that you marry cannot remain the same person for the rest of their lives. That would result in a stunted life.

In God's perfect plan, as you would expect, man and woman were made for each other; made for a partnership. Almost as if they were the two halves of a circle so they beautifully complement each other when they are joined together.

Woman has an inner reality which is lacking or subdued in most men. It is an inner reality which makes sense of so much of life itself. Man can support this with his outward bias. He is ready to take on the world outside.

Add the two together, the inner reality and the outward bias, and you have two people, complete as one. When both are in harmony with God's eternal purpose then you have a circle headed heavenwards.

The differences

Women, however, often seem to make the spiritual discoveries in life ahead of men. Part of the explanation lies in the very way in which men and women are structured.

From school age onwards boys generally advance ahead of girls in those areas of mathematics which involve abstract concepts of space.

Boys usually show superior hand/eye co-ordination and perform better at the sports which need this. This same advantage enables the man to construct three dimensional objects from two dimensional line drawings.

The better spatial ability of men certainly helps to explain male superiority in map reading. The experiment has been repeated on many occasions with the same results. Girls and boys were given city street maps and without rotating the map were asked to describe whether they would be turning left or right at particular road junctions as they mentally made their way across town and back again. The boys always did better.

I watch the walkers on the Coast to Coast long distance walk as they come through my nearby town of Kirkby Stephen. More women than men like to turn the map round, so that it physically matches the direction in which they are travelling.

If the male brain seems to give men the edge in dealing with things and theorems there is no doubt that the female brain is organised much better than his to respond sensitively to all sensory stimuli. Women are better than men in tests of verbal ability. The woman, it appears, is better equipped to receive a wider range of sensory information. She then connects and relates that information with greater skill. Women place a higher value on personal relationships and communicate better than men do. Cultural influences and intelligence may and do reinforce these strengths but there is evidence that the differences are innate.

These differences give a woman a bias towards the spiritual side of life. Add the fact that the events of birth involve the woman much more deeply than any man and you are on the road to understanding why women often find faith first in a household.

For the wife, conversion brings a new thrill to life; a new dimension, a new reality and a comprehensive answer to the meaning of existence. The husband, on the edge of things and possibly under pressure in his work, treats it all with mild disdain or tolerant amusement.

The wife has discovered a personal God. One who is worthy of her adoration and worship. If in romance days she, 'worshipped the ground that her husband walked on', then now she has found someone really worthy of such treatment.

Sooner or later it is going to show. Men may not notice for a long time and then, when they do, they become angry. Sometimes all hell breaks loose. They are angry at themselves for not having discovered this secret of life before their wife. They feel slightly out-manoeuvred. They are angry that this new found faith is now taking up time and receiving attention which used to come their way. They are also angry because of the deep down fear that this conversion has marked the beginning of the end in the relationship.

Now most men are not very 'intuitive'. It isn't one of their strong points. But men do sense when they are being left out of things and often, like spoiled children, they react with a tantrum.

An extra dimension

Of course, in one sense, they are right. Until they, themselves, become a follower of Jesus Christ with their wife, then they can never be quite as close again. Once they do make that decision of mind and will they are bonded to their wife in an extra dimension; that of eternity.

If you can picture the bottom line of a triangle. The husband is the left hand corner and the wife the right hand corner. When they both worship God as believers, they both move in the same direction; towards God at the apex of the triangle. Their journeys trace the two side lines of the triangle. They are heading upwards closer and closer to God as each day passes. But something else is happening as the triangle of life is being formed. As they move individually closer to that top point so they are moving closer to one another.

This is the true eternal triangle.

What if only one partner is heading for God? Well at the best the unbelieving partner will be attracted and at least mirror what the believer is doing. So they won't get any further apart. You get a parallelogram picture. If on the other hand the second partner grows more self centred whilst the first grows more Christ centred, then the two get further apart instead of closer together. One heads upwards and the other downwards. They do not form a shape and as time goes by the couple will grow further apart on the very basic reasons for being alive.

One thing that I have discovered is that man does not like to be left behind. Take a silly example. Put a man, even the most mild mannered of men, behind a steering wheel at a set of red traffic lights. On this side there are three lanes of traffic on the other side of the lights the road narrows to two lanes. Watch the reactions of the men in the front grid position. You'd think it was the Grand Prix. Listen to the squeal of tyres. Men do not like being left behind; being beaten is not appreciated.

Now here is a very serious point. I have observed it myself and many people have written to me about it. When a wife discovers faith and gets converted she, in effect, leaves her husband behind. She has won the race to find out what life itself is all about. We are here on earth in order to know God in heaven so that we can live with Him for ever. That sounds so simple but is so profound. Jesus used slightly different words saying,

For God so loved the world that He gave his one and only Son, that whoever believes in him shall not perish but have eternal life (John 3:16)

If the wife gets there first, then the man in question finds it very hard indeed to accept her discovery. In many other areas of life, men are reluctant to admit that their wife was right after all. I have heard furious arguments in my own home as I stoutly defended the indefensible rather than admit that my wife was right. So you can understand how difficult it is for the man to come to terms with his wife's conversion.

If it has all happened as a result of the wife going along to the mums and toddlers group and meeting other women with a real faith, then the man can write it off as women's stuff. If it is a result of some brilliant sermons preached by the handsome new curate then he, the husband, feels jealousy rising as he feels his attractiveness as a leader is threatened. We are into a competition mode of living. There is no way in which this husband is now going to admit that he needs this religion. The Devil-made macho man takes up his position.

Take the early opportunity

We have discovered that there is an early opportunity in the first few weeks after a wife has made a commitment to Christ when the husband will listen to a sensible presentation of the Christian message. It is probably asking too much to expect him to come along to church. Anyway, you can't repeat the meeting which resulted in his wife's conversion. That was a special guest service with a gifted visiting evangelist. Now you are back into the routine Sunday service pattern again, possibly following some deep devotional teaching for mature Christians.

Our advice to church leaders is simply this. Whenever a wife comes to faith, take the opportunity within the first month to talk to her husband about what it is that she has believed. Do it in an environment where he feels at home. If he plays golf then play a round with him. If he enjoys a drink, go to his local pub with him. Take some risks in order to win him. At least give him the opportunity to turn the invitation down. When you explain the faith to him talk to him about discovery and leadership. I'll say more about that in chapter 6. You are offering him the chance to catch his wife up before she reaches the first bend in the track. Then he can stay ahead of her in the race of life. It is far more important than I can ever explain. Give him the chance to take the lead. If you don't do it, then as the days go by, it will become more and more difficult for him to accept the fact that his wife was right after all.

As well as making the effort to answer his questions and explain the faith to him in man's terms, you should concentrate all your prayer power upon him in these early days. Don't start praying for him only when his wife wants to become a member of the church. Start now, as soon as she is converted. Concentrate prayer on everyone around him – neighbours and friends, work colleagues and team members of any sports club that he belongs to. The aim is to win them all. The key to winning him may be when one of the men that he admires becomes a believer.

Marriage with an unbeliever

I have had a few letters where the wife was a believer before she married her unbelieving husband.

I have to say that this seems to be in direct conflict with the stated word of God.

Do not be yoked together with unbelievers. For what do righteousness and wickedness have in common? Or what fellowship can light have with darkness? What harmony is there between Christ and Belial? What does a believer have in common with an unbeliever? What agreement is there between the temple of God and idols? For we are the temple of the living God (2 Corinthians 6:14–16).

Some Bible commentators suggest that this Scripture passage can be applied to business partnerships. I certainly know of a lot of stress and strain which Christians could have been spared if they had chosen a Christian business partner for their venture. But all the commentators, from John Calvin to the modern day, take the word 'yoked' (the Greek word is *Zugos*, a heavy burden) to refer to the harnessing together of two lives in marriage.

Don't you sometimes feel that your partner isn't pulling their weight in some area or another and that you are having to carry the heavy load yourself?

If, as a believer, you chose to marry an unbeliever then you were starting out on the most difficult of all journeys with a huge extra problem. In a marriage between two believers there is an apex to their marriage triangle. God is their common goal. So as life progresses and they both get a little closer to God, they are at the same time both getting closer to each other.

There are many problems in marriage and many books

are written on the subject. Christian marriages are not free from the stresses and strains caused by unemployment or shortage of finance or high mortgage rates or the birth of children.

Not every Christian marriage is free from the pressure of poor housing or family interference. Not every Christian couple finds sexual harmony easy to achieve. There are a thousand problems in marriage without having the basic one of standing on different ground in relationship to God.

When a Christian woman and an unbeliever marry they are in fact standing on different planets; she on heaven and he on hell. Different planets move in different orbits and usually go different ways. Trying to hold hands across such a space divide is asking for trouble.

The trouble usually arrives after about six or seven years of marriage and one or two children. The birth and bringing up of the children often brings the wife back to a deep faith in God. It puts her in touch again with other Christian mothers in one of the local churches. She begins to realise just what she has been missing.

The husband starts to resent her involvement. Many pour abuse on the need for a crutch to life. Some deliberately use the name of Jesus as a swear word in order to be one up on the wife. The wife wakes up one day to feel that she has very little in common with the man that she married. The truth is that she never did have much in common. They were never standing on common ground, not even on the same planet.

To the unmarried woman who says to me, 'I've fallen in love with him,' I reply, 'Then fall out of love.' It isn't easy but neither is it impossible; it involves your mind and will taking charge of your emotions. However charming or handsome or odd the man is (some women do fall for odd-looking men!) there will be others like him. In reality it is a 'type' of man that knocks you off your feet. So wait for another one whose faith matches your own and whose love for you and for God will bind you closer together when the storms of life try to blow you apart.

To the woman who tells me that she will win him for Christ after they are married, I have to answer that my thirty five years of evidence stands against her assumption. In the hundreds of examples that I have heard about, the hard fact remains that if he hasn't become a believer before you get engaged then you won't be any more successful at winning him after the wedding.

Marriage with a backsliding Christian

I have a handful of letters in my file from women who feel that the man they have married has gone back on the faith that he seemed to have before they married.

What do you say about the issue of backsliding? Let me suggest two things. The first is the promise of Jesus concerning those who are truly his own:

My sheep listen to my voice; I know them, and they follow me. I give them eternal life, and they shall never perish; no-one can snatch them out of my hand. My Father, who has given them to me, is greater than all; no-one can snatch them out of my Father's hand. I and the Father are one (John 10: 27–30).

They can fail to listen to the voice and go their own way bringing wasted years, but Jesus speaks of having a hold upon them which cannot be broken. If they are in a state of backsliding then all you can do is to pray.

My second word of advice is this. Don't let their lack of Christian vitality suppress your own. Don't allow their lack

of fire to put out yours. I believe that the most likely thing
to set them on fire again is to see the flame of God burning
brightly in your own heart. That doesn't mean spending
all your time at religious meetings, but it does mean living
close to the Lord.

The death of a partner

What about the husband who has died? He didn't attend
church and sometimes a widow's grief is compounded by the
question of what has happened to him now. The honest
answer is that we must leave such a question in the hands of
God. I have been surprised how many men have had a faith
which their wives never recognised. For many men it is not
Christ who is the problem, it is the church that puts him off.

I have also personally known a man who came to faith
in his closing days as he died from cancer. He was my own
father. In his early days he had attended Sunday school and
maybe in those years put his trust in Christ. It certainly
never showed in the years that I knew him as an adult but
in those closing hours there was no doubt that he trusted
alone in Christ for eternal salvation and that God, in His
amazing mercy and grace, received him into the Kingdom.

A serious question

It is time now to put a very serious question to those wives
who have an uncommitted partner.

Do you really want him to be converted?

One letter from a wife whose partner was still uncommitted raised an intriguing issue. 'We have come to a happy
arrangement about Sunday morning,' she wrote. 'I take the
children off to service and my husband cooks the Sunday
lunch. He quite enjoys this one adventure in the kitchen

and he's become very talented. I have realised that if he gets converted and comes along to church as well, then we have problems over the lunch.'

Yes indeed, not everything will be easy when he becomes a Christian. Another letter told of certain marriage difficulties that this couple were encountering. The wife hoped that he would get converted and it would solve the problem. It was clear even from the letter that she, more than her husband, would have major changes to make in order to keep the marriage going and that his conversion would highlight the need for those changes in her attitudes.

It might disturb the equilibrium if he became a Christian. It might also disturb the church. Our observation is that when older men come to real faith then they often want to know why the church hasn't been making the message more available to men like themselves.

They begin to challenge the church's use of its resources and the level of commitment of the membership. The Christian wife then moves from the position of everyone being sympathetic because her husband is an unbeliever, to people starting to avoid her because her husband is stirring things.

Many wives also have an intuitive feeling that if he is wholehearted in his new found faith it will change the family life-style as well. Serious tithing may well replace a few coins from the housekeeping purse. He may want to give away the second car to a missionary couple home on furlough. There may be no stopping him if he really gets converted.

So I ask my strange question, 'Do you really want him to get converted?'

One lady wrote of how her husband came home from a men's dinner to tell her that he had seen it all. It had all suddenly made sense. Her reaction was to burst into tears and say 'I'll have nothing to pray for now.' Incredible!

There are certainly difficulties in living with a man who is all out for God and our experience is that when a mature man becomes a Christian he does tend to go all out for God.

But of course you want him converted. You want him to share in the things of eternity. You want the family to be one in Christ. You want him to take up the leadership role in your home and in the Kingdom, that God designed him to have.

Is it time to start claiming some of your husband's ground for the Lord? In my office I have a banner which says,

'I will give you every place where you set your foot' (Joshua 1.3).

It is a promise from the Bible.

I am sure that there are places where your husband wants to go or sometimes needs to go – events like the firm's annual dinner. Far too many Christian wives start to run away from such opportunities. 'I don't feel at home there any more,' said one of them to me. Well, I can understand that. But instead of declining the invitation and making your husband feel that you are becoming a religious fanatic, why not claim that ground for the Lord?

You don't have to drink at these events. You can do the driving. If you pray about it beforehand and if you get two friends to pray for you whilst you are actually at the event, then it might turn out to be a place for Christian witness.

What if your husband's managing director says to you, 'I've noticed you seem much more at peace with the world these days, Ruth. What's your secret?' What an opportunity and what a privilege. At some of these events you may be one of very few real believers present. Is God trusting you with that privilege?

Perhaps the Lord wants that opportunity taken in order

to influence others who also need to find faith. You could demonstrate God's power in that place. Remember to claim the promise in every situation: *'I will give you every place where you set your foot.'*

Let's go back to the ideal. Both partners are believers; as they live for God so their lives are more closely harmonised with one another. In a Christian marriage the husband is striving for the ideal spelled out to him in the Bible.

Husbands, love your wives, just as Christ loved the church and gave himself up for her to make her holy, cleansing her by the washing with water through the word, and to present her to himself as a radiant church, without stain or wrinkle or any other blemish, but holy and blameless. In this same way, husbands ought to love their wives as their own bodies. He who loves his wife loves himself (Ephesians 5:25–28).

Here is a lovely thought. As a husband cherishes his wife in Christian love so she is prevented from the ageing process! Without wrinkle or blemish, and looking far better than with any special cosmetic face cream. Every man wants to have a wife like that!

So how do we put the message into ways which he will hear and understand? You see, not all men are alike.

Chapter 4

Not all men are alike

Not all men are alike. And they are certainly different from women. I don't just mean in biological functions, but also in attitudes and expectations.

Having looked at the evidence I believe strongly that the concept that men and women are only different because they are culturally conditioned so to be, falls down under careful examination.

In childhood, in politics and in fashion, men's and women's tastes are different. Why should we feel that one presentation of the Christian message is appropriate for both sexes? We are not changing the message but we do need to present different facets of the message – and there are many facets to our amazing message.

The light will shine for women when certain things are highlighted. Indeed it has already shone for them brightly. That is why we have so many of them in our churches. What happened was that the preachers felt that they had got the whole message in those themes; after all people, albeit mainly women, were responding. When men didn't respond, we rationalised the matter and said that the men were harder, they were even Gospel hardened.

The real problem was that we were Gospel illiterates. We

were broadcasting the message clearly to the women but had not even begun to think through the issue that women and men might hear things differently.

The woman's way

In all of our research into how women have become Christian believers, the issue of need has arisen time and time again. Over sixty per cent quoted some aspect of need or even crisis as a major factor in their conversion.

The majority of the remainder were women from churchgoing homes who were in the church environment. These heard the message of Jesus often in their early years and it seemed right to make a response.

The crises included personal illness and marital problems. Sometimes the family had been hit by tragedy in the form of a death or the serious injury of someone close. It is possible that women are affected by the crisis earlier or more deeply because they are closer to the event and spend more time caring for those involved. Many of them did not have a full time job or career to divert their attention from the sense of grief and loss or loneliness.

One woman wrote of her, 'sense of desperation for "someone" to help when facing the probability of being diagnosed with multiple sclerosis.' Here are some other case histories.

'I had endured a very traumatic year including close death, domestic problems and other serious factors. I knew I needed to rely on something bigger than me.'

'There was unresolved grief following my brother's death, brought to a head by my parents moving from the family home town where my brother is buried.'

In all of these cases there was frequent mention of the help, support and gentle witness of Christian friends during the times of crisis. The Christians went in to help and showed that there was a power beyond human resources and these women turned to the God that they saw in their friends.

Then there were scores of other need situations. Often it was expressed as a desire for something more to life. More meaning or more purpose was sought. A longing for more love or more joy in life itself. Then there were the fear needs; fear about the future or death or just a felt need for security.

Again it would seem that the sense of need is triggered in women at an earlier stage because they reach the point of emptiness sooner.

The men's way

There is a major difference between men and women over admitting need. The man is determined not to admit need which he equates with weakness, at any cost. He can then often stave off the emptiness more easily by his involvement at work or in his hobbies.

Professor C Cooper, professor of management at the University of Manchester Institute of Science and Technology, has been doing some research into how people cope with stress at work.

He found that comradeship and support at work help women to cope with stress, 'but the men do less workplace "counselling" because they see their colleagues as competitors and rivals rather than friends. Men fear that any admission of weakness may be used against them in the promotion race.'

There is a very clear distinction between the woman who has enough courage and common sense to admit her need and the average man who is determined to go it alone.

When faced with the increased risks of cancer because of

his heavy smoking the man simply shrugged. Pressed by his doctor to say what he was going to do about the danger of shortening his life, the man replied, 'I don't let myself think about it.'

So we pick up one of the clues as to why men have not been responding to what we thought was a clear presentation of the Christian message.

Our message, for years and years, has been a message of need. You need Jesus. You need the love of God. You need forgiveness. We have come at it time and time again from the angle of need. The women, who are closer to the realities of life and prepared to admit their need have heard us and responded. The men have not even heard. Need does not figure in their vocabulary. They simply shrug it off.

There are a small number of men in our churches who became Christians after their marriage and who still have uncommitted partners. Most of these women turn out to be the stronger personality in that home and the men are sensitive men who have responded to the need message.

I believe that an important factor in the evangelism of men is for preachers of the message of Jesus to stress some of the other tunes and truths of the Gospel rather than keep on playing the symphony of need. I will look at how to do that in the last chapter of this section and then give some guidelines for practical ways to gain a hearing for the message in chapter 8.

A man's make-up

Let me now help you to see some of the basic building blocks in a man's make-up.

Men are not good at words.

There are, of course, always some exceptions, but by and large, girls learn to talk earlier than boys. Did you know that boys outnumber girls by four to one in most remedial reading classes? It's the boys who have most difficulty with the words. Stuttering is almost exclusively a male complaint.

Over thirty years ago, psychologist Herbert Lansdell discovered that men and women, damaged in the same area of the brain, were differently affected. Working at first with epileptics, he found that men with brain-damage on the right side did badly in tests relating to spatial skills. Yet the relative performance of similarly brain-damaged women was scarcely affected. The men lost all their capacity for spatial IQ tests, the women did not.

Herbert Lansdell moved on to the left hemisphere. Men with left-side brain damage lost much of their command of language but women with damage in the same area retained most of theirs. Men were three times more likely to suffer from a language problem than women. Lansdell came to the conclusion, now generally accepted, that in women language and spatial skills are controlled by centres in both sides of the brain but in men such skills are much more specifically located. Numerous studies have since confirmed these early findings.

So women use both sides of their brain for verbal ability. The man mainly uses the left hand side. That's why the men are not so good with words. I didn't say that is why women talk more.

Communication

The couple had come for marriage guidance counselling. Their marriage had hit a rocky patch, most marriages do from time to time, and this couple needed help. It was obvious that the man did love his wife and wanted the marriage to continue. Her complaint, however, and it was justified, was that he never told her that he loved her. She lacked the security of his affection.

We told him that he must tell his wife that he loved her. Every day he must say, 'I love you.'

Guess what he did? He went home and cleaned his wife's car for her. I mean cleaned. It was washed, shampooed, waxed and polished. The inside was cleaned, vacuumed, the upholstery brushed and the windows gleaming. It was in immaculate showroom condition. He was trying to show that he loved her, but he couldn't say the words.

Now that raises an important issue. Much of our Christian faith is expressed in a very exclusive form of church language. We have developed a special vocabulary. We have an in-built set of jargon words. In its extreme form it can be used to keep a certain church as an exclusive club which you can only enter if you pay the entrance fee of learning the right words. You can observe this in some conservative circles where the King James Bible reigns supreme and at the other end of the spectrum in some bouncy charismatic circles where they refer to some subjects only by the initials of the words needed. Both are exclusion zones.

Just what does a man have to say before he can be admitted as a believer?

A minister told me that for the last six months he had been meeting face to face with one man for a Bible study. But that the man was not yet a believer. I didn't think much of that minister's gift of evangelism. Actually, what he meant was that the man hadn't said all the right words in the right order.

Here is a woman in Eastbourne who has been a Christian for many years. Her husband is a scientist and she longs for him to be a Christian. She wants him to be able to say that he knows 'with absolute assurance and clarity that the precious Lord Jesus Christ is his very own personal Saviour and that the blood of Jesus, alone, has washed away all the filthy rags of his sin.'

Now, please, don't think that I am mocking her, but I am deeply concerned. She is laying down rules which the early church did not find necessary. She will wait an awfully long time for her husband to say words like that. They are our modern (not so modern) jargon words. Her husband doesn't know words like that. Please don't mistake lack of jargon for lack of faith. When I talked to that scientist, the witness of my heart and spirit was that he was a believer after all. He put it this way. 'I have crossed the line, you know.' That was C S Lewis's lovely phrase, and he'd read a lot of C S Lewis.

The early church required a man to say that, 'Jesus is Lord.' and then to demonstrate by his actions that he was on the Lord's side. Don't go adding to what God may require of a man. In fact, I recommend to wives who feel that they have uncommitted partners that they ask someone in their church who has a recognised gift of discernment to give them a second spiritual opinion on their husband.

We have discovered that there is sometimes a reinforcement of unbelief in a husband because of the attitude of the Christian wife. Don't keep telling him to say the right words. Listen to what he actually is saying. Perhaps he should be treated as a baby believer rather than an unborn child.

One man whose job is in sales told me that, 'From now on I'm committed to the product.' Praise the Lord, I thought. But what I said was, 'Great, I'll get you a copy of the sales manual.'

Out to kill?

Let me uncover another of men's secrets.

Men are competitive.

Oh you knew that, did you?

'He even competes with his own son!' one lady said in amazement. But, of course, that is how men are made and that's how the son tests out his strength. I have just watched a father and son playing chess. It went on for hours because neither would give way; one of them had to win.

Man's competitive aggression gives you some understanding of why men rarely have any close male friends. It has nothing to do with the fear of homosexuality, it is because they compete all the time. These two men play golf together on a regular basis. I tell you plainly that on the fifteenth green it has become a needle match. Two young men who live near to me often have a game of squash. On court they seem out to kill one another. Because aggression is stronger in men than in women, wives who become Christians really do need to watch what they say about Jesus.

One very attractive young woman went home after an evangelistic presentation at which the message of God's love had been brilliantly explained. She was a new person. She told her husband that she had, 'fallen in love with Jesus.' Now I know what she meant but it was not the best way to put it to an athletic and aggressive man. He turned up at church demanding to see this Jesus. He intended to thump him. In many cities there are lots of foreign names; Jesus must be just another bloke.

'Not for me'

Now here is another of the barriers that we must overcome if we are to get men to understand the good news.

Men don't want to be hypocrites.

'Going to church,' said John, 'is for believers and I'm not yet a believer so it wouldn't be right for me to go to church.'

John had a very real point there. He wasn't just being awkward.

If you look at the early chapters of the book of Acts, it is obvious that the early church was a gathering of the believers. Those who were really committed to Christ *'were called Christians first at Antioch'* (Acts 11.26).

These early believers were so committed to one another that *'they shared everything they had'* (Acts 4:32).

The general public clearly did not go along to church in those early days; indeed, *'No-one else dared join them'* (Acts 5:13).

The word used for church is the New Testament Greek word *ekklesia* from which we get our English word 'ecclesiastical'. It means 'the called out ones'. The Christians were people who had been called out from darkness into the light of God. They had been called out from the Kingdom of the evil one into the Kingdom of Jesus. They were called out from failure to faith.

So it does logically follow that church is for the believer. I have every sympathy with the man who doesn't want to be a hypocrite by going to church. I do feel though, that we have every right and the responsibility to invite him along to hear about the revolutionary Christian message. I want to do that in informal home meetings or through sports events or special interest activities which give an opportunity to get to know each other or in a restaurant setting with a meal and an after dinner speaker talking about the Christian faith.

It isn't a get out when a man says that he doesn't want to be a hypocrite. Let's set up a whole series of informal stepping stones towards faith for men. I want to see churches running a lot of Christian events which are not religious in their trappings and setting.

Do you have an Agnostics Anonymous group? This offers

an opportunity for men to talk to other men about their questions concerning life and death matters. Men need a great deal of support in this modern world and the Christian men should be giving a lead. It might mean that some Christian men will have to pull out of religious committees in order to have time to meet with the uncommitted men who have real questions to ask.

Awkward situations

Men are easily embarrassed.

For many men who haven't been to church very often, maybe never since they got married, church is seen as a place where it is easy to be embarrassed because you may not know what to do or when to do it.

'Oh, that really isn't true,' one minister said to me, 'men are not put off that easily. They are much braver.' I took him along the high street near to his church and invited him to go into the betting shop; I knew he had never been into it in his life. He declined my offer to pay for any bet that he placed.

What was the problem? It was twofold. Someone might see him going in; and once inside he wouldn't know what to do and that would mean that he would have to ask for help from someone else.

Men don't like asking for help. That is why I get my wife to ask for travel directions when we get lost in a new town. I know that she doesn't always remember complicated directions easily but then neither do I, and if she has asked I can blame her when we get lost again!

That's what men are like. They don't like being embarrassed.

We were on our way to Sunday morning service. The man that I was staying with had persuaded his neighbour to come along to the special guest service. His neighbour was a local magistrate and a very talkative man.

I was driving my car and the neighbour and the man I was staying with sat together in the back. 'What's this special speaker like then, Roger?' he asked my host. He didn't know that the driver was, in fact, the speaker.

I pricked my ears up. How would Roger describe me? Roger didn't hesitate for a moment. 'He's great,' he said. 'One of the most entertaining speakers I've ever heard.' I grew two inches in the front seat. I couldn't get any taller because now I was already touching the roof. I couldn't wait to hear myself speak that day.

The conversation went on to other less important things but our neighbour was clearly ill at ease about something. As we reached the church car park, it reached the surface. 'Roger,' he said, 'you will help me find my way through the book, won't you?' Light suddenly dawned. The last time this man had been to church had been for a formal 1662 Prayer Book service, and there is nothing worse than losing your place and being on the wrong Collect for the day. His hesitation was because men are easily embarrassed. He didn't have to be helped through the book at that church because they had a printed, short, order of service and the songs came up on the overhead projector screen. He described my talk as 'interesting.'

Men don't want to feel that they may be embarrassed; church is often seen as a place where you can get embarrassed because you don't always know what to do.

It happened to me in a church that I was visiting. It was the notices time and you know how your mind wanders during the notices. Then all of a sudden everyone was standing up and I was left sitting down.

No one had announced the fact but at the end of the notices they always brought forward the collection which had been taken just before the notices. When they did that, they always stood for a prayer. Everyone knew, except visitors like me. Now any woman who was visiting would have picked up the signals out of the corner of her eye that people were getting ready to stand up and she would have stood up with them as if she knew exactly what to do.

It is actually a fact that women have wider peripheral vision than men. The woman has more of the receptor rods and cones in the retina, at the back of the eyeball, to receive a wider arc of visual input. How many little boys have been caught out in the classroom by being seen when they thought they were unobserved? 'It wasn't me, Miss!' is answered by an unequivocal, 'I saw you do it!'

The woman sees it all and acts accordingly. We men, with our blinkered vision, can get caught out and fail to stand up when we should have done. It was most embarrassing. I had to pretend that I was picking something up off the floor which I had just dropped.

Show your courage

Just one more insight into men's attitudes.

Men are always looking for strength.

We really do need to work much harder to show just how demanding the Christian faith is for modern man. Don't play down the challenge of it all; spell it out.

Here is an incident from the home of a young woman who became a Christian some months ago. At first her husband did the standard male thing in regard to her new found faith: he closed his eyes and hoped that it would go away. But it didn't go away; it was a real conversion to Christ.

Then the man in question began to resent his wife's involvement with the church. 'I don't want you to go out on a Wednesday to that midweek meeting anymore,' he announced one day. Well, it wasn't the end of the world if she didn't go. The church actually recorded the midweek meeting and so she could listen to the tape on Friday.

Then her husband told her that she wasn't to have any of her Christian friends round in his house. It was actually 'their' house but he claimed the right to lay down the law and it wasn't worth a big fight. She could go round to her new friends' houses for an occasional coffee.

Then this man began to find things that they must do together on a Sunday morning like visiting the new theme park or going on a special shopping trip: things which stopped her getting along to church every week. She began to feel the pressure.

Finally, the day came when he came home from work and told her that she had to give up 'all this Christianity lark.' She had to choose between him and God. If she chose God, then he was leaving her.

It was at that point that she showed her bravery. 'I don't go out on Wednesday,' she said, 'because you asked me to stay in with you. I haven't had my Christian friends round to the house and recently I've missed a few Sunday services because of your plans. But I am not giving up my personal faith in God for you or anyone else. It is too important.'

You know what? He has treated her with respect ever since that confrontation. He was looking for strength. He had decided that there was nothing in this Christianity. So he was pressurising his wife. Give this up; give that up; give it all up. If he could have made her do that it would have proved that the whole thing was empty.

But he found that there is a power in the believer and a courage that comes from their God, and he recognised it. He's not converted yet but he makes room for her Christian commitment and he has met some of her Christian friends.

He did also go along to an informal meeting to hear a Christian sportsman talking on the subject 'Scoring goals for Jesus.'

Perhaps it is time to look again at the way in which we present the Kingdom message to men.

Chapter 5

The male challenge

Christians have the best message in the whole world but, often, the worst presentation imaginable. We are just not putting the message into words which men can understand.

We so often style our talks like *Sunday Times* journalists when the average man reads the *Sun*. We present our message like a BBC 2 documentary programme when the average man is watching 'The Match'.

We seem to have lost any sense of urgency and the spark of excitement. Both the challenge and the fun have gone out of our faith.

When did you last hear a preacher as excited as a sports commentator? One of the reasons why we have not attracted or affected the men in our country is because we have concentrated on preaching a message to women and have not faced up to the male challenge.

A major part of our failure has been because of the way in which we separate our church life from the world of work. Faith is what you do for one hour on a Sunday, just one day of the week. Work is what takes up sixty hours of the week (counting travelling time and overtime) and may cover six days of the week. Indeed, for many a man, his work takes up more than half of his waking life.

The real world?

Almost every church that I visit has separated the world of work from the world of religion. In a recent church prayer meeting, the people who attended were asked to pray about problems facing a missionary in Asia who had visited the church once for a deputation meeting. They were then asked to pray for a native pastor in South America whom they had never seen but whose name had come up in the magazine of a missionary society. But they didn't pray for the deputy headmaster who was present in the meeting itself and who faced major pressures over the local senior school budget. Nor did they pray for the young woman starting with a company as a graduate trainee engineer. Nor did they pray for Jean's husband who will be made redundant if his firm doesn't get a certain government contract. The man outside of our churches sees unreality in all of this. It is one of his reasons for saying that the church is full of hypocrites. He isn't saying that we are not sincere but that we are actors. *Hupocrites* is the Greek word, and it means those who play at life.

Men have two basic needs. Neither of them, despite all the jokes, is sex. Men need love and they need work. Work usually takes priority over love; work gives man his identity and his status.

Freud summed it up: 'Work gives a man a secure place in a portion of reality, in the human community.'

So it is not only our words that will need to be changed, but also our emphasis, when it comes to prayer meetings and sermon illustrations.

A recent study by Alice Deakins analysed the topics that men talk about. Deakins found in her 'eavesdropping study' that when there were no women present the men talked mostly about business and never about people, not even people at work. Their next most often discussed topic was food. Another common topic was sports and recreation. When women talked alone, their most frequent topic was people – not people at work so much as friends, children, and partners in personal relationships. The women discussed business next and thirdly, health, which included weight control.

The Jesus way

So men have a fixation about the world of work. Is that why Jesus in his ministry and teaching majored on subjects from the world of work and is that why he drew crowds of men around him?

In the official parable teaching of Jesus you will find that he refers to the world of work four times more often than to the world of home and family. His illustrations come from pragmatic incidents rather than heavenly theories. Yes, he does say,

God is spirit, and his worshippers must worship in spirit and in truth (John 4:24).

But on that occasion he was talking one to one with a woman. Women have a spiritual awareness that is lacking in men.

Did Jesus present the message differently to men than to women? It is worth looking again at some of the incidents in His life. Let me give you one example to start you off along this kind of Bible study research. In John's gospel, at the start of chapter 8, he records the occasion of a woman caught in the act of adultery.

You will remember the setting. Jesus is teaching at dawn in the temple courts, presumably in the outer court where women and gentiles were allowed. He has been doing this for some days and so the teachers of the Law and the Pharisees set a trap for Him.

They bring a woman caught in the act of adultery. 'Moses' law,' they say, 'commands us to stone such women. Now what do *you* say?'

Jesus is sitting down. That was the position the Jewish teachers of His day adopted when they wanted their words to be noted down as official teaching. Jesus did the same. An example of that is the Sermon on the Mount, given when Jesus had sat down to teach – you can find it in Matthew 5.

For the Pharisees, the woman caught in the act of adultery raises the question as to whether Jesus taught and affirmed the law of Moses. If He doesn't, then clearly, He cannot be from God. The crowd would immediately leave and look for another Messiah.

If, however, Jesus does uphold the law of Moses and support the death penalty by stoning, the Pharisees could immediately report Him to the occupying Roman authorities and have Him arrested: in an occupied land only the Roman governor had power to order an execution. Even the chief priests in Palestine had to go to Pilate to ask permission for a death warrant when they wanted Jesus killed.

So they thought that they had cleverly trapped Jesus. Presumably one of them, or a paid accomplice, had taken the woman to bed so that they could catch her 'in the act of adultery'. It is strange just what lengths authorities will go to when their power or prestige is threatened.

Jesus, sitting down, now bends down. Is it a sign of humbling Himself still further? Is He weighed down beneath the sins of the world? Does He write, 'Father, forgive them for they do not know what they are doing'? Or is He wrapping a cloak around the woman to protect her from the stares of the men and the early morning cold?

The incident ends with Jesus looking into the eyes of the woman and saying,

'Has no-one condemned you?' 'No one, Sir,' she replies. 'Then neither do I condemn you,' Jesus declared. 'Go now and leave your life of sin' (John 8:10–11).

What a marvellous message of forgiveness! The Saviour doesn't say that we can live how we please; the sin must be left behind. He does say that there is forgiveness even for those who have been caught in the very act of sin. What a message of grace and hope! But who heard that message? The women heard it. All of them, the woman caught in adultery and the other women who had been in the crowd listening to Jesus' teaching. Women in those days were not allowed to throw stones.

The men didn't hear the message of forgiveness because they had all left. Every one of them had gone. Jesus had said to them *If any one of you is without sin, let him be the first to throw a stone at her* (John 8:7).

What the men heard was a clear message of conviction and condemnation, and a challenge to right living and loving. The men had all been reminded that they were all sinners. Even if they hadn't been with the woman, they had at least thought about it and,

Anyone who looks at a woman lustfully has already committed adultery with her in his heart (Matthew 5:28).

So the women heard one message, and the men heard a quite different one. Take a look for yourself at some of the other incidents in the ministry of Jesus and see how He tailor-makes His message for men and women. Let me suggest some other areas where we should start asking ourselves, 'Does this theme appeal more to men or to women?'

1) *Jesus as a friend*

If I speak about loneliness and answer that need by talking of Jesus as a friend, I suggest that it is the women who will hear me gladly. They are the ones who are more likely to admit their need. More men than women prefer to be loners. It is the young wife on the housing estate, shut in with her eighteen month old baby who feels lonely. Her husband commutes up to the city for work. He leaves before seven in the morning and gets home after seven at night – British Rail and weather permitting.

He has had a busy day at work solving problems, talking to clients, planning with his colleagues. The wife is the lonely one who is ready to see Jesus as the friend who never leaves you on your own. You are not supposed to talk to yourself but it is quite legitimate to talk to God. We call it praying and you can pray out loud in your own home on your own if you want to. You realise that you are not on your own, and then you can't be lonely.

I am suggesting that this frequently preached theme is biased towards success amongst the women.

I have even heard the Good Samaritan parable spoken of in terms of friendship and never being on your own, when it could equally be interpreted as a corporate company rescue bid. The man was obviously on business going from Jerusalem to Jericho.

If, on the other hand, my preaching can stress that God is with us to guide us, then maybe that slightly different emphasis will raise an interest in men. Programming, planning, plotting are all 'men' activities. Let's tell the men that God has a master plan for our universe. It is a masterly plan. It is the Master's plan. Even more thrilling is the fact that God has placed in our world the power of His Spirit to get things done. That mighty Holy Spirit, that Spirit of power, can dwell in our lives when we become followers of God's only Son, Jesus Christ. There is some evidence that 'signs and wonders' evangelism has resulted in more men coming to faith as a proportion of total enquirers.

'Jesus in my heart bringing comfort' is a word to a woman. It appeals to her sense of inner reality. 'God the Holy Spirit in my life bringing the power to get things done' is a word for men. It concentrates on the outer, visible, concrete world. Perhaps we ought to get back to the biblical emphasis on Jesus as Lord and Saviour and the Holy Spirit as the Indweller who turns us into God's Overcomers.

2) *Emotional release*

If I minister a lot on the theme of release and the emotional release which you receive when your sins are forgiven, then I suspect that it is the women who will hear me most readily.

There is a great freedom which is received along with salvation. There is a very real freedom from guilt and fear and it can have a clear emotional effect, especially on a woman. 'I was in tears', one young woman said, 'thinking about the cross and what Jesus had done for me. How He had loved me, and that. I just wanted to love Him in return.'

Perhaps my ministry ought to stress Jesus as King, alongside the truth of Jesus as Saviour. Indeed maybe the word 'redeemer' is more balanced than 'saviour' and perhaps then I will be addressing the men. The emphasis in the Bible is not just on being saved from sin but rather upon building the Kingdom of God. Men hear that message more clearly.

Stress the fact of living as a *colony of heaven* (Philippians

3:20) and remember that Jesus' first recorded message was *The time has come. The Kingdom of God is near. Repent and believe the good news* (Mark 1:15).

Again it is interesting to note in the Marc Europe survey *Christian England*, that in the new House Churches the ratio of men to women is often nearly equal and has remained steady. If there has been one theme at the top of the agenda of the new churches over the last twenty years it is the theme of 'the Kingdom of God'. They sing it with confidence. 'We declare that the Kingdom of God is here'. Have you noticed that the men sing the line first in that Christian song?

3) *Repentance*

Take another look at repentance. We have to talk about this matter. It is a fundamental to the Gospel message. Peter in the very first church sermon of all time says, *Repent and be baptised* (Acts 2:38), and again a few days later, *Repent, then, and turn to God* (Acts 3:19).

If I stress repentance as our sorrow for the failure of our lives then women are much more likely to understand because they have often wept over failure; their own and others. If I emphasise the other, equally valid, side of repentance, not what I turn from, but what I turn to, then I suggest that I may be heard by many men. Repentance is a turning to God's way. My message to men tells them what they were made for, and the things that they are to do.

He will do even greater things than these, because I am going to the Father (John 14:12): repentance opens up a new dimension on life. Christianity is not then a prop for weak men but the key by which strong men discover the meaning to life itself. Repentance means involvement in restoring God's broken image in our world.

Commitment to the message means action to back up the

words. There are injustices to put right and protests to
be led and maybe even laws to be challenged. Don't expect
your men to be happy sitting in rows looking at the back
of people's heads. The women may like to sing about
the church triumphant; men want to be the church
militant.

4) *The world of work*

If my ministry is home centred and most of my illustrations
come from the world of the family, then I will find a listening
audience amongst the women. We are in a difficult area here
because most ministers do have their study and office in
the home and so are surrounded all the time by family life.
One minister decided to try opening an office down at the
church hall.

Unfortunately, the hall was used four mornings a week
by the mums and toddlers. So he swapped one mother and
two toddlers for twenty eight mums and hordes of toddlers.
His sermons continue to be filled with illustrations about
children.

In case you write to remind me of Jesus' words, *Let the
little children come to me and do not hinder them* (Matthew
19:14), remember that the mothers had brought them for
a blessing and that Jesus didn't stay around after He had
placed His hands upon them.

The times when Jesus used a child as an illustration was
to demonstrate a fact to His disciples, not to make a point
to the crowd. Jesus' emphasis was consistently on the world
of work.

Maybe if I take His example and stop divorcing the world
of work from the life of faith then the men will hear me more
clearly. In some churches the leaders don't even know what
jobs the other leaders do on weekdays. How can you pray

effectively for each other if you don't know what takes up the largest single portion of time? The world of work is where man is competition orientated. Perhaps we ought to remind modern men that the church is involved in the biggest competition of all, the battle between light and darkness – and we Christians win in the end!

5) *Use of words*

Let me repeat my concern over our misleading use of words. Thoughtlessly we have alienated many men in this way. The phrase 'receive Jesus into your heart as your own Saviour' is one which will appeal to women but which has a built-in alienation factor for men.

Place your emphasis instead upon the challenge to men to follow Jesus as Lord. Man always wants to do things himself. Of course, in the realm of eternal salvation, he cannot. We can remind men that it was the perfect man – the GOD/MAN, Jesus Christ, who has achieved our salvation. It was the GOD/MAN who won the victory and we can participate in that victory by praising God and following Jesus Christ.

Here is a fact about man. Man needs status and man is given his proper position in our world only when he is linked to Christ. The male challenge is one which we must take up immediately. Jesus did say that He would draw men to Himself. He also said,

When you have lifted up the Son of Man, then you will know that I am the one I claim to be and that I do nothing on my own but speak just what the Father has taught me (John 8:28).

That lifting up to die was clearly meant as a demonstration

of the truth that he was the GOD/MAN, the 'I AM' of eternity.

Even as He spoke those words many put their trust in Him. Have we failed men by not declaring the actual truth concerning the GOD/MAN? We have spoken of Jesus as a friend, a helper, a healer but undermined His deity. Jesus is the magnificent. Jesus is man as man was intended to be. He was God's man on earth. What man lost by sin, Jesus, by His activity, has reclaimed for man.

The first man, Adam, gave up his God-given authority to the devil, in the Garden. That action turned the garden into a desert. But look what Jesus has done. Jesus went into the desert and wrestled the authority back from the Devil, turning the desert back into a garden. 'When you eat of the tree,' God said to Adam in the garden, 'on that very day you will surely die.' But Adam didn't die that day. He did eventually die, but it was many years later. The person who died when Adam sinned was Jesus. Jesus died on the desert hillside and was laid in a tomb in a garden.

The fact that Jesus was thousands of years after Adam in history does not affect the fact in eternity. With God, there is no time concept. 'A thousand years are like one day.' It was the same day that Adam ate that Jesus died. Sin is matched by salvation. It is man's unique place in the plan of God which is revealed by Jesus' unique death within the purposes of God. Jesus is the GOD/MAN who replaces dying with living:

For as in Adam all die, so in Christ all will be made alive (1 Corinthians 15:22).

Have our churches got a serious health problem? Have we failed to stress that in the original plan of God, man was to be God's man and God's leader on earth. Jesus, therefore, restores what God intended man to have.

To the extent that we have neglected our good news for men, we have failed to be the Kingdom of God. It is time to reaffirm what God wants. I believe that as we rediscover the place of man in the plan of God we will see increasing numbers of men begin to follow the perfect man, the GOD/MAN, Jesus Christ our Lord.

Section Two

Evangelism for men

Chapter 6

How most men think some of the time

How we behave in any given situation is clearly influenced, in part, by the role stereotypes set by the society in which we live.

How we react to certain words and activities is affected, in part, by our previous experiences of life and by our life expectations.

I have often had to gently coach a man about which piece of cutlery to use for which course of the meal when he is faced by a formal dinner setting where all the pieces of cutlery are out at the same time. There seem to be so many to choose from.

Do these stereotypes influence men's reaction to our presentation of Christianity? They most certainly do, and we ignore that fact at our peril.

Dr Peter Trower in a paper on the differences between men and women wrote:

To play a masculine role, you are supposed to be, for example, independent, unemotional, assertive and logical.

To play a feminine role you are supposed to be, among other things, dependent, talkative, emotional and home-orientated.

Not every man and woman feels right about every aspect of the assigned role and many resent the social expectation that they should conform to it.

Surveys and observations, however, reveal that most men and women accept these stereotypes.

Such stereotypes clearly place religion and religious faith, as it has been seen in recent years, in the area of competence for the woman. We have strongly reinforced this idea to the men by presenting our message as an aid for weak people who can't cope and need someone to lean upon along the road of life. Men have more important things to do.

Baby boomers

A recent research report by James Eagle and Jerry Jones explored the special characteristics of men born in the period between 1946 and 1964. These men, especially the first batch born just after the Second World War, are sometimes referred to as 'baby boomers'. There was a boom in the birth of babies as men returned to their wives after being away on wartime duties.

One of the main conclusions of the report is that baby boomers are a generation with different values. They are entrepreneurial, they are men who want to get things done. They tend to look for and desire instant gratification. Does this explain the success of the McDonald's food chain?

These men have a greater tolerance for diversity. The development of a multi-racial culture has been taken in their stride. In this respect it is fascinating to see that other faiths have spelled out their distinctiveness whilst Christians have often played down the unique claims of Jesus Christ to be the only Saviour.

Baby boomers tend to resist rules and set ways of doing things. Maybe our orderly services where everything is predictable and bland have been a turnoff to these men. Would that explain the fact that a larger proportion of men are attracted to the charismatic and pentecostal forms of expression and worship?

Finally, it has been shown that men of the baby boomer generation will contribute money and time to worthy causes. There is a whole generation of men around in their thirties and forties who are looking for some cause worth associating with. It must demand their all. It must be worth dying for. It has to be the Christianity that we have failed to make clearly known to men.

Let's take a look at some other areas where men demonstrate different attitudes to those of women. It will help us to discover some clues on how to present our amazing message of eternity to modern men. Along the way we will have to acknowledge that some of the things that we have been doing in our churches have actively discouraged men from getting involved with God. If we had wanted to put them off, we couldn't have done it better.

In our churches we have effectively and efficiently divorced the world of work from the world of Christian faith. That has been one of the worst things that we could have ever done.

Let me remind you of the quote from Freud mentioned in the last chapter. Freud correctly analysed man's need for work. Here is what he says:

Work gives a man a secure place in a portion of reality, in the human community.

Take a careful look at those words; 'security', 'reality' and 'community'. For a man, they all relate to the world of work.

The woman, by and large, finds security in her relationship with a man as husband or lover. She finds reality in childbirth and community in family. All of our presentation of the Christian message is geared towards helping her find her place within the love of God. Virtually nothing that we do shows a man how to find his eternal place in the work plan of God.

Attitudes to emotion

An analysis of women's magazines, both the traditional ones aimed at women who have chosen marriage and motherhood as a career and the newer magazines directed at women working outside the home, has recently been completed.

All the advice offered in the main articles tended to have some psychological content. For one group it was understanding oneself, one's children and one's partner. In another the emphasis was on insights into oneself and one's male and female colleagues and superiors at work.

Men's magazines on the other hand, tend to stress performance – business, sports and sexual performance – rather than insight.

In the women's magazines, the fiction explores problems women face in their daily lives. The men's fiction is characterised by action and adventure and conquest.

If you want to know how a woman felt when she knew that she was pregnant or going to be a grandmother or how she coped when she lot her job at the age of fifty, it is all there in black and white to be read in the women's magazines.

But if you want to know how a man felt when he learned that his baby was a girl or why he can stay for hours in front of the television set when the World Cup is on the box, you're less likely to find out. On the whole men don't talk about these things. Nor are they generally interested in reading about how other men think and feel about such subjects.

We will turn in a few moments to this major difference in emotional attitude between men and women but first let me reinforce a suggestion made in chapter 3 to those women who have come to faith but whose husbands do not, as yet, share their faith.

Please don't let your faith, and new-found interest in the church, cut you off from your husband's world of work. Claim your husband's ground for the Lord. Take all the legitimate opportunities that come your way to be involved in any work based activity. Encourage your church to organise a dinner for men with an after dinner Christian speaker who is an acknowledged expert in your husband's type of work. Kick-start one of the men in your church into inviting your husband along to the event. Get as many people praying as possible, all around the world, and give God a chance to show that He is interested in your husband as a whole person. For the man, that includes the vital sphere of work. It is work which gives so many men security, reality and community.

What place is there for the emotional side of things in our presentation of the Christian message to men?

Deborah Tannen in her book *You Just Don't Understand* explores the different conversational styles and what she calls the unspoken 'metamessages' sent and received by women and men.

While admitting many individuals are exceptions to her general conclusions, she identifies a number of ways that male and female conversational styles tend to differ.

Women's conversation, she says, tends to be 'symmetrical' – emphasising equality and intimacy – and is judged primarily on the basis of how close the participants perceive themselves to be.

Men's conversations tend to be 'hierarchical' – emphasising each person's independence and relative status. In groups, men tend to identify who has the best information on the topic of interest and grant that person an elevated status.

Thus, while women judge conversations by the quality of interaction, men gauge conversation by the quality of the information. Linguist Tannen calls it 'rapport versus report'.

Intimacy versus awe

I want to suggest that in our churches we have talked too much about being close to God and not enough about standing in awe of God. We have built a case for intimacy which the woman has responded to gladly, but we have failed to speak of the mighty acts of our God; acts which affect man and his destiny.

We have deliberately given men the impression that our God is the one who comes alongside to help in times of trouble. We have failed to declare that our God is the shaper of the universe. We have not told men that God sits in the heavens and laughs at man's puny attempts at running the world. We have failed to spell out that man can be God's man, working to the master plan.

Men perceive emotional love as an area of weakness. I've often heard women admit that they 'need a cuddle' but I have rarely heard that from a man. Give him a manly embrace and you do, in fact, get through to a different dimension but the emphasis there is on the strength involved in the bear-hug not the comfort of touch.

Caring love has also had a bad press in men's minds. Caring for the less fortunate and for those with handicaps of some form or another has been seen to be women's work. Quite rightly, the women in our churches have played a leading part in caring. Our churches have been a source of refuge for some of the less adequate souls whom society brushes aside in its rush for success.

We have forgotten the fiery words of God's prophets who challenged nations concerning their treatment of the defenceless. It takes a man of faith to move a mountain of indifference. It takes a man of courage to challenge the status quo. It requires a man of enormous power, power beyond his own human resources, to stand against the forces of indifference, corruption and self interest to get things changed for the better.

We have been lop-sided in our presentation of the facts and as a result men have associated Christian love with weakness. Emotional love and caring love have been seen as women's work. Men have to get on with the 'real work' in the world.

I have to raise the question of whether the 'gift of the pastor' is characterised by stronger female elements. Is a pastor, by nature, more inclined to see things from a woman's point of view?

Peter Wagner defines the gift of pastor as, 'The special ability, which God gives to certain members of the Body of Christ to assume a long-term personal responsibility for the spiritual welfare of a group of believers.'

Is the caring role of a pastor, that of acceptance and support? Is it the prophet's task to stand up and challenge the world or the government or both?

If I am even partly right, then it is easy to see how ministers and clergy taking on the pastoral role in the church would feel threatened by having too many strong men around. Prophets would threaten their priestly and supportive function. They would then have an identity crisis. The simple solution, unconsciously performed, is to continue to present the message in ways that will produce a response from women without getting too concerned about whether the men are hearing the message in ways which they can relate to as men.

Strong love

We do not have to play down the great fact that, God so loved the world. Love is the demonstration of God's activity. God's love is to be seen as a demonstration of His energy. It is seen in creative and dynamic work action, not simply as an emotion emanating from the heart of God.

God's love is commitment to a plan and an outworking of a purpose. These are the elements which man sees as representing strength.

We have linked faith to a perception of weak love instead of strong love. Perhaps we need to hear a little more about the steadfastness and power of God.

I am increasingly convinced that if we are to present the message of Christianity to men in a meaningful way then we must stress that faith is linked to discovery and to power.

The Christian invitation to men is an invitation to be men again; men as God intended man to be, in control of the earth and in contact with heaven.

Becoming a Christian, for a man, involves a radical change for the better. It means replacing man's modern madness with the sanity of faith.

Men, I have observed are much more biased towards being 'doers' rather than 'hearers'. It is time to show them what they must do in order to be a disciple instead of spending all of our time telling them what they must believe.

I have observed another interesting difference between men and women. Women are more likely to enjoy sharing their troubles without necessarily expecting any answers. They will talk about the issue or the problem without producing any solution. Men, however, are much more likely to focus immediately on how to solve the problem.

Here is another incident recorded by Deborah Tannen. Her request was for men to record a telephone conversation with a friend. One man insisted that he didn't have telephone conversations with his friends.

'Don't you ever call John on the phone?' he was asked. 'Not often,' he replied. 'But if I do, it's because I have something to ask, and when I get the answer, I hang up.'

Another woman's husband produced a tape with great satisfaction and pride. 'This is a good conversation,' he announced, 'because it's not just him and me saying things like "Hi, how are you? I saw a good film the other day," and stuff like that. It's a problem-solving task. Each line is meaningful.'

When his wife listened to the tape, she heard her husband and his friend trying to solve a computer problem. Not only did she not consider it 'a good conversation', she didn't really regard it as a conversation at all.

A man's idea of a good conversation is often one with factual, task-focused content. The woman's good conversation is usually one which had personal content.

How many sermons do you hear which tell you how to go out and revolutionise the world? Maybe a few more would attract a few more men.

Blind faith

Furthermore, many men feel that faith is illogical or at least argue that Christianity lacks proof.

It is clearly a perceived view that those of us who are Christian believers are unthinking and gullible and have been taken in by some unsubstantiated religious theory.

Coming, as I do, from a background of careful analytical research, I find it amazing that anyone should think that we Christians have been easily taken in. But we have given the impression to the man in the street that there is little hard evidence for Jesus. I will deal with some of the evidence in a later chapter.

Let me briefly introduce the question of proof. Can the Christian faith be proved? Yes, there is empirical proof, that which the evidence supports.

Men in particular want things to be logical. It is no answer to argue that man is himself a walking contradiction; a machine that somehow holds together despite the odds. Men say that they want rational facts not emotional feelings, and then often react in highly emotional and immature ways.

'You can't prove Christianity!' one man said to me. I patiently took the time to show the evidence for Jesus Christ. I called upon the testimonies of men from down the ages who had put the faith to the test and discovered that it worked. I added a little of my own story and what had happened to me that very week and, at the end, he said, 'Oh, I didn't mean prove it that way.'

What *is* proof, we might ask? You cannot completely prove the theoretical link between heavy smoking and lung cancer but all the evidence points the same way and says that there is a clear connection.

There is a logic about the Christian message. It declares a purpose for life itself. So much within us cries out for a meaning to life. Christianity gives a constructive world view. The time has come for some power-speaking from the churches of our land. My research indicates that men respond to clear words and strong opinions. I am not saying that they all respond by believing, but they are quite clear about what they either do respond to, or they are quite clear about what they reject.

Organising the church

In our churches we are still not organised to bring about the revolution of faith in men that our generation stands poised to make. Many of our church structures are based on leadership models which are now obsolete and are certainly not New Testament in origin. The hierarchy of many churches is generally based on models learnt in wartime military conflict. They pass orders down from the top to the troops below. Not many men want to be part of that. Men want to be the chiefs not the Indians.

The new role model for the progressive and growing church needs to be that of an orchestra. Every member is a brilliant musician in his own right; capable of solo performances and able to teach others. What holds the orchestra together is that they are working from a common score and watching the baton of the same conductor. Christ alone is able to beat time in time with eternity. He is the one to whom we must look and when we look to him we find that we are in harmony with one another. The Church of England may represent the string section, the Salvation Army the trumpets and the Pentecostals the percussion but there is no doubt that denominational alliances such as we have today will soon be as outdated as dinosaurs.

Just as our funny religious jargon is outdated already. No wonder men have difficulty in understanding the dynamic of our message when we have wrapped it up in 'thee's' and 'thou's' and 'whatsoever's'.

Many Christians seem to have lost their ability to speak in plain words. Just as too much television can apparently reduce a family's ability to talk to one another, so too many church meetings where the audience (sorry, congregation) just sit there, seems to deaden their ability to be able to talk on the wavelength of their non-Christian friends about their faith.

In the airports of life, the Christians walk through the green channel. They have nothing to declare.

You may have heard of 'doublespeak'. It is the upmarket word for jargon.

Did you know that in America (America always leads the way) a lift operator in a big store is now called a member of the vertical transportation corps?

You can go out nowadays and buy an 'experienced' car – a second-hand one. On television we watch 'encore telecasts' – the same old programmes repeated again. In the world of doublespeak dying is 'terminal living'.

By the way, has your favourite dentist told you the proper name for a toothbrush? It is a 'home plaque removal instrument'.

But we have lots of jargon words in our churches and, if anything, it is getting worse. The end result is that the outsider finds it more and more difficult to find a way in. In some churches the jargon factor is deliberately encouraged to keep people out. These churches only admit the ones who want to be jargon clones. The ones who work hard enough at accepting and understanding and imitating the right style, prove by doing so that they will not be disturbing influences, and are permitted to enter.

Speaking in Christian jargon has had a place in church history and may do so again. In the Bible, in the book of Revelation, John uses a whole series of coded words as he refers to Rome and its Emperor.

But the church in the United Kingdom is not currently

under persecution at all. It has its greatest opportunity this century to spread its message amongst men. It needs to learn how to state strong opinions and how to use clear words so that men have to face the claim which Jesus Christ makes upon every man's life.

For the man who wants to be different we have a message:

Then Jesus said, 'If anyone would come after me, he must deny himself and take up his cross and follow me' (Matthew 16:24).

For the man who wants to be radical we have a message:

Jesus said, 'Go, sell everything you have and give to the poor and you will have treasure in heaven. Then come, follow me' (Mark 10:21).

For the man who wants to change the world we have a message:

Jesus sent them out with the following instructions: 'The kingdom of heaven is near. Heal the sick, raise the dead, cleanse those who have leprosy, drive out demons. Freely you have received, freely give' (Matthew 10:7–8).

We have been gender blind, broadcasting our message in terms that women have understood and not asking ourselves the hard question about whether or not men were hearing at all.

Chapter 7

What every woman should know

I believe that men are the fragile sex. Women are the ones with strength of mind and purpose. In adversity it is so often the woman who stands firm and tall. In matters of faith, women are frequently way ahead of their male partners.

It is possible to identify at least five clear stages in the way that men grow up. If you are a wife who has already found faith, then understanding how your loved one matures may well help you to be more in step with him through life. If he is not yet a believer then you will learn in this chapter some of the 'opportunity-moments' which God will provide.

God never gives up on a man and in this life a man will have many second chance times to believe in God and receive eternal salvation. There is, within every man, a child. At every stage of life that child may reappear. We often see that as a problem but you must remember the word of Jesus,

I tell you the truth, unless you change and become like little children, you will never enter the kingdom of heaven (Matthew 18:3).

The first phase of adult man's growing up is the period from

eighteen through the twenties and thirties. They are the
onward and the upward years.

These are years of great struggle; not so much for survival
as for status. They are tension-ridden years when men are
concentrating on establishing themselves, possibly in three
areas at once. The pressure turns a man into a triangular-
shaped man. He is under pressure to perform and establish
himself at work, in his marriage and amid family
responsibilities. Have you noticed how up-tight men
become about performing?

The world of work is a competitive jungle. Save some
sympathy for him when he gets home after slaving all day
over a hot computer.

Establishing a role

In his marriage he is also developing a role and an image.
He is trying to live up to the image of an ideal husband
which childhood gave to him. This may be a copy of his
own father but is more likely to be the portrayal of the ideal
man which he received from his mother. Or maybe he is
trying to be the dream husband that he thinks his wife wants
him to be.

If children come along during this period, then he tries
to prove himself as a father as well, trying to be as good
as, or better than, his own father was perceived to be. So
you can see how he may be pulled in three different
directions at once. He can be stretched at work, as a husband
or as a father. If you stretch a rubber band in three ways
at once then you put it under tension. Immediately the
tension is released the band jumps back to its smallest size.
That is sometimes a man's reaction to the pressures of these
years: he acts like a small child again.

So in early years men run hard; they have to, in order

to keep up with things. Their interests lie in their families and in getting ahead on the job. They push themselves to win promotions and salary increases. This single-minded dedication takes its toll. Men who at twenty radiate charm often seem colourless, hard working but bland at the age of thirty.

In various interviews, men have been asked what they need from their wives during these difficult early years. What kind of support would they like from the identikit, ideal wife?

The answers all come down to the same thing. They want their wife to be a 'mother figure' to care for them and comfort them. At the same time they want her to be a 'film star figure' so that all their male colleagues are amazed that you have married him. Finally they want their wife to be a 'Joan of Arc', a strong woman, capable of fighting and winning all their battles for them. Who said that men were not dreamers?

The consolidation years

These onward and upward years are followed by the thirty-five to mid-forties era.

My description for this second period is to call them the consolidation years.

Man is concentrating, sometimes very hard indeed, on establishing himself. He builds on previous achievements. If he is in teaching, then this is the time that he becomes a head of department or a deputy headmaster. In industry, he might move company and take on a major promotion at the same time. If he is in charge of a big concern, this is when he gets a large salary increase.

You don't have to look hard to see the stress possibilities. Occasionally a man is promoted beyond his capabilities and then there is trouble. In the old days such a man was quietly moved sideways in the firm. Nowadays, he is likely to end up redundant.

The pivotal decade

Then at forty or forty-five or even later, man enters the crucial decade. Some writers call it man's pivotal decade. I am talking about the male mid-life crisis.

Traditionally the age of forty has been seen as the psycho-social marker for men. The birthday adverts in my local town paper are always geared at the fortieth birthday, often with a picture of the man from when he was a young boy.

Man senses the arrival of middle age, characterised by physical and psychological symptoms.

Just as for a woman it doesn't all happen in one month and then no more periods, for the man this time can run on and on. The bad news is that it can take a man up to ten years to get through this mid-life crisis time. The good news is that he will come through.

Middle age arrives earlier for men than women for the simple reason that men have a shorter life expectancy. Up to this mid-life point man thinks mainly about the years that he has lived. Suddenly, sometime around forty, he begins to think about the number of years he has left to live.

That crucial transition is marked by a mental change from thinking, 'If I die,' to thinking and eventually saying, 'When I die'.

At the same time he begins to re-evaluate the things that he has done. Almost without exception, each man feels that he has achieved very little for all the years that he has spent on earth and that now his time is running out. Men begin to long for some great adventure.

That is what makes it 'crazy ideas' time. He comes home

and says, 'Darling, we're going to sell up down here and buy a farm on the Outer Hebrides and live a self-sufficient lifestyle for the rest of our days.' Then he walks away! The wife is left reeling from the implications. What about Granny? What if the children were ill? Where are the Outer Hebrides anyway? She knows, and her husband knows that he doesn't know anything at all about farming. It's a wild idea caused by mid-life crisis.

Being the practical woman that she is, she will make contingency plans and read up on farming. Then a fortnight later she discovers that he has forgotten all about the Outer Hebrides; now he wants to buy a bed and breakfast place in Cornwall.

A man called to see me a little while ago. His wife told me that he had this crazy idea. He introduced it to me as a great commercial opportunity. He had plans to start up a mushroom farm in the south of France. I asked him how old he was. 'I'm forty six,' he replied. 'What has that got to do with it?'

You know, don't you?

Mid-life time often sees an increase in drinking amongst men. I don't mean going over the top, but he needs a drink more often to cope with the inner conflict. One lady in Surrey summed it up exactly. She told me that they bought a bottle of wine now and again to have with their dinner at home. 'We used to have a glass each and put the rest in the fridge, but now he finishes the bottle.'

The other clear symptom of this pivotal decade is the compulsion to escape the ageing process. If he has been a keep-fit enthusiast, he is unwilling to admit that he cannot now do all the things that he used to do. He will push himself unnecessarily and harder than he should in order to postpone the day when he has to admit that he has got older.

In business, this is the time when he takes his young secretary out for lunch. There may be no element of romance or sexuality in it at all; he is just trying to prove that he is still attractive to younger women. The statement that he is making is that he is not growing old.

Towards retirement

When he comes through the crisis, he moves into his fifties and on towards retirement. This can be the sensible decade.

The period of fifty to sixty-five can contain years of great peace and stability. Of course, if he never comes to terms with who he is, then there can be a residual bitterness. For most men, however, these are stable years and many marriages have some of their best ever times during this period of life.

Traditionally at sixty-five, but currently often much earlier, modern man takes his retirement.

We need to remind ourselves that retirement is a modern phenomena, a new experience for men. Men are not used to retirement. In the good old days, they just didn't come home from work one day. They became frail or had an accident at work and that was the end of their life. Men didn't retire, they just died. At the turn of the century, the average life expectancy for a man was only forty-eight and for a woman it was fifty-one. Actuaries who work out pension schemes for the future are now working on an average life expectancy for men of eighty and for women of eighty-four.

Times have changed. We live longer, we are generally fitter and we retire earlier.

Retirement can be taken very young nowadays. I talked to a bank official who had been offered an extremely attractive retirement package at the age of fifty-one. Being a cautious banker, he asked me if he should take it. The problem is, you see, if you take away his work, then who is he?

A man can be known as 'George in the stores', or as 'our best salesman'. A man can be introduced as 'our head of research' or 'the man in charge of our overseas operations'. If he loses his job he may even lose his personality.

An anthropologist speaking to a group of business executives' wives said, 'Women can enjoy an irreversible achievement by giving birth to a child. Men have nothing like that. The only way men can realise themselves is through their work.'

The man who comes to terms with his mortality through faith in Jesus Christ, enters retirement with a growing sense of satisfaction and serenity. The man who never comes to terms with the facts of life may continue with resentment and disappointment and even sheer fear.

I stayed in the home of one such man, a medical doctor who had conducted some interesting research during his working life. He exuded anger. The medical profession had never rated his work highly enough, according to him. Now he no longer had the laboratory facilities to carry on his research. His mind was active but his hands couldn't complete the process and he was destroying the life he had left. He needed a miracle of God's grace to happen in his inner being.

I have also observed how many men turn their retirement hobby into a job in order to give themselves status in the real world.

One man told his wife that he was looking forward to retirement because then he could really do all the gardening he had always wanted to do. He was keen on growing vegetables and took on an allotment area as well as the garden. Well, two years after retirement he has succeeded with the vegetables. He grows so many that the family and neighbours and friends cannot keep up with eating the supply.

So now he has negotiated a deal to sell fresh, 'organically grown' vegetables through his local supermarket. He has turned his hobby into a job, because the job gives him a purpose in life, and purpose brings meaning into life, and meaning brings security.

Adapting to the ages of man

What Christians need to see is that all of these ages of man give new opportunities to present that man with the Christian message in a way which will make sense to his life at that time.

During those onward and upward years there will be crisis times. I am not suggesting that you should pray for such things to happen in order to get him converted but be aware of the opportunities that these crises provide.

Injury at sport to anyone who has been a keen participant raises the question of human frailty and gives God a chance to break into a busy life during the recuperation. See that he is supplied with some good Christian books and videos.

Illness has the same effect and provides similar opportunities. Why not register with a Christian doctor in order to be ready?

The loss of a male relative through death, one's father, or brother, or even a business colleague, is also a crisis time for a man. My wife recently attended the funeral of our neighbours' son. He had died suddenly in his thirties. Business friends and university colleagues were present at the service. They listened to the preacher more carefully than they had ever listened to a preacher before because death had impinged upon their carefree life-style.

Most ambitious young men seem to acquire a mentor towards the end of that upward and onward stage of life. Psychologist Daniel Levinson writes, 'The mentor is usually eight to fifteen years older. He is old enough to represent greater wisdom, authority and paternal qualities, but near enough in age or attitude to be in some respects a peer or an elder brother. He takes the younger man under his wing, invites him into a new occupational world, shows him around, imparts his wisdom, sponsors, criticises and bestows his blessing.'

Such a relationship is usually short lived, no more than a period of three years and then the younger man has to assert his own authority and be his own man. We need mature Christian men who are not tied up with the routine of running the church so that they can be free to act as mentors who will introduce men to Jesus Christ.

How about a club just for men to share some of the pressures and some of the answers that men have discovered? Launch it with a Christian doctor talking on the subject of stress.

Capitalising on consolidation

When you move into the next period, that of consolidation, then at least three second chance opportunities present themselves.

Every man longs to be a good father to his children. Even the worst of men has an inner longing to be a better father. When a child is born, especially the first child, it is not only the mother who goes through an enormous physical and emotional upheaval; the father does as well.

The hospital telephoned me to say that my wife had given birth to our son just an hour before. I was thrilled, but then came the reason for their call. My wife had suffered a severe haemorrhage and they wanted me to be with her.

Within minutes, I was at the hospital. They dressed me in a hospital gown and gave me a mask to wear and took me straight through to the delivery room where the medical team were working hard on my wife's behalf.

As we went in we passed the cot where baby Geoffrey had been placed. He was fine and all the medical attention centred around my wife. But I was rooted to the ground by the side of the cot. The nurse thought that I had run out of courage to see my wife, and came back to encourage me. But it was the sight of a three dimensional photograph of myself that had stopped my progress. I had seen photographs of myself as a tiny baby, and here in the cot was a living, breathing, moving replica.

The birth of a child has a profound affect on a father. Churches should not be waiting for parents to approach them about bringing the child to church. Send your congratulations cards out as soon as you see the announcement in the local paper. I assume that you have got a key worker delegated to the task of picking up local news which can be used to provide opportunities for the Gospel.

Then invite that father and any other pregnant (prospective) fathers to an informal home group to talk about, 'How to be a good father.' No one is running advice clinics on this issue, so you can take the lead in your community. Use the video made by James Dobson in the series 'Focus on the Family' as one of your evenings together. It is called, 'What Dads need to know about Fathering.'

Consolidation years often involve a change of location; either because you can now afford a bigger house or because the starter home that you bought is now too small for the growing family; or maybe promotion for the man involves a move to a new town.

See it as a great opportunity to start together in a new place with a new group of believers. One man's promotion has taken him from the south east up to York. Because of difficulties in selling their house the family have needed to remain in the south whilst he lives during the week and some weekends in a hotel paid for by his new employers.

We made the suggestion to him that he could look around in his spare time to find a church that his wife and children might like to attend when their house is eventually sold and the move completed. He knows that his wife goes to a quite charismatic church and so he has been checking out the services at all the charismatic churches in and near York.

You see he isn't doing it for himself, is he? He's just carrying out some research. I'm convinced that his house down south hasn't sold yet because he needs to get converted on one of these church visits first.

Losing a job

Sadly, it might be unemployment which hits a man during any of these periods. The new company may go out of business or the established enterprise might be taken over. Nothing is sacred nowadays: even my old company ICI has been threatened by takeover.

When a man loses his job it is a traumatic time. Churches and church leaders are then given one of the greatest opportunities for social caring and evangelistic ministry that they will ever have in that man's life. Have you got someone with the gift of the evangelist, who can visit these men? They are now available in the day time. Maybe that's why one of your own church leaders was made redundant.

Is the church office available so that the man can use the

photocopier at cost to send out copies of his curriculum vitae, or use the telephone to make calls to potential employers? Is there some helpful job that he can do on the church premises or church grounds in a voluntary capacity? It needs to be in proper working hours, leaving home at his usual time in a morning.

You have to give the man some dignity again. You have the opportunity to tell him that, in God's sight, he is valuable as a man and that God wants his help in building the Kingdom. I have come to the conclusion that churches are missing out on these opportunities to reach men who are made redundant. It is often because ministers do not understand what it feels like to become redundant. Find someone in the church who has lost his job in the past and give that man the task of ministering into this situation.

Please don't misunderstand me. I am not in favour of unemployment and I am not advocating that we should pray for more of it. But I am pointing out that such a crisis time in a man's life provides an evangelistic opportunity if we are ready for it.

John had built the company up over the years that he had been with them and was now the senior manager of his area. The take-over was not unexpected and John felt that it would be for their greater good, but within weeks all was in turmoil as their new owners sold them on to an American concern.

This manager was then told by the new company that they had rationalised their European network and his division down in the West Country was no longer needed. He was told to work out redundancy terms for the forty strong workforce and inform them immediately.

He worked long hours and got the best deal that he could for his men, some of whom had been with him for years.

Then he got a telephone call from Head Office. They were

pleased at his efficiency, but now his services were also 'surplus to strategic personnel requirements in the current climate'.

John knew that at his age he wouldn't get another job at that level of management. Over the weeks he learnt that he wasn't going to get any offers at any level. At first it was fun to be home and a relief from all the pressure. He did all the jobs around the house that he had promised to do over the previous two years. For the first time in his life he had time to think.

He thought about God. What is life all about? Why are we here at all? He had been running so fast to keep his place in business but now it had all evaporated within a month. There must be more to life. Thank God that a godly Church of England minister has led that man to Christ. The crisis was redundancy and it provided an opportunity – a second chance time.

Opportunities at mid-life

It is obvious that mid-life time is also going to be a major time of Christian opportunity. Man is asking questions. He feels his fallibility. He is conscious of time and eternity as never before. The big questions are forming in his mind. 'Who am I anyway?' 'Why do I exist?' 'What is life meant to be for?' 'Is there something beyond death and can I know about it?'

Every man has a mid-life crisis. If he reached for the stars he now knows that he isn't going to get there. He wanted so much to fly and now he's come down to earth. Make sure that Christian wives and teenagers are not blind to what is happening to Dad. Make him a key member of the family again. Commend him as a man as often as possible.

Sometimes the couple have settled into different

compartments of life. His wife has now been a believer for some years. She is accepted at church and a member of various committees. The teenage children play in the church worship band. At mid-life time Dad comes to the conclusion that they might, in fact, have something which makes sense of life. He'd like to ask a few questions but none of them is ever around in the evenings any more. They are too busy with their Christianity. Don't miss the opportunity.

The transition from thinking 'if I die,' to 'when I die' really is traumatic. Especially when a man thinks of how much he had hoped for from life and how little he feels he has accomplished.

Sometimes, at this stage, a man will dearly want to turn to his family but finds it impossible. Partly because he cannot put his need into words and partly because no one responds to his silent calls for help. In the onward and upward years man concentrates on the job success. He goes through all the motions of being a good father. He attends parents' nights at school and goes to the end of term concert, but he often spends little time talking to his children.

When he turns to the family in his mid-life crisis the family are simply not there. His children are completely involved in their own lives, their activities and friends. His wife is busy going from one meeting to another.

For the man in their lives, there is no room in their lives.

He makes a few fumbling attempts to reach out to them but it is all so unexpected that the change is not recognised by anyone. So the little boy emerges again. 'If they don't want to play with me, I don't want to play with them.' Remember that if he acts like a child, that gives him a chance to find a childlike faith. Please, Christian wives, don't miss the opportunity to help your husband at mid-life time. Introduce him to the real game of life. Make father a key member of the family again. Commend what he does and affirm him as often as you can.

This is a time to concentrate your prayers on prodigal fathers, praying that they will come to their senses and come home.

Mid-life time is a time when Christian families can be too busy to see their father's need but the Father in heaven sees it.

Opportunities in retirement

Then we must look again at retirement. Prince Charles has done his best to encourage the 'oldies' by explaining hopefully that, 'The third age offers an interesting opportunity; the postscript to the long letter of life; it is, or could be, the final glorious, concluding paragraph.'

Strangely many people nowadays seem to see retirement as more like a hectic footnote to fill up any space at the bottom of the page. Is that an indication that they are not prepared for the 'fourth age' of eternity?

Analysts have also come up with a strange factor concerning retirement for men.

There is a peak in the male death-rate about two years after retirement. Irrespective of the age at which retirement is taken, there is a peak death-rate two years afterwards. The men just seem to rust out. Work so absorbs a man and gives him such a structure and reason for living that, when it is removed, the whole building of life falls down.

It takes courage for a man in his late fifties to face the fact that soon he will be entering the last stage of his life. Man must then take a good look at his position; financially, physically and emotionally. It also becomes an opportune time to look at the spiritual dimension of life.

Some companies run very effective pre-retirement courses

for their employees. As well as dealing with the practical matters of ageing most of these courses aim to encourage men to think positively about their 'third age'.

In order to enjoy it fully, they suggest, you should look for new friendships. You will need, at retirement, a whole new circle of friends, new ambitions, new horizons, a new reason to go on living. What better time could there be than this to introduce men to the reality of faith? A whole new group of friends called the church. New ambitions – to be God's man on earth. New horizons that stretch to eternity itself.

What Christian wives should realise is that they have more influence at the start of retirement than at any time since courtship days. Just remember what he was willing to do in those days!

Men who tended to disregard their wife's advice in earlier years are now astonishingly ready to follow a lead from their wife. Men will go along with most decisions or suggestions that she makes regarding everyday activities. Train your older women to be gracious and winsome. Don't allow the Devil to trick them into thinking that their husband has become 'Gospel hardened.'

Retirement planning has to be one of God's great second chance times for men. There are plenty of practical subjects to talk about, all of which have spiritual implications.

Your Christian financial consultant talks about pensions and making your money work for you. Your sports person talks about getting fit without pain. Your health food shop manager about how to lose a few of those excess pounds of weight. Don't let the secular professionals be the only ones working in these areas.

Did you know that it is easier for a man than for a woman to lose weight? Forty-one per cent of a man's body is muscle compared to thirty-five per cent for the woman. This higher proportion of muscle to fat, combined with the fact that muscle burns up five more calories a pound than fat does, just to maintain itself, makes it easier for men to lose weight.

So you have the start of your callanetics club for men based on scientific facts.

Let's be excited about the future second chance times which are coming our way. They will give us opportunities to present the Christian message in a way that relates to where men are at each stage in their lives.

Chapter 8

Practical ideas for reaching men

Ever held an apple pie night? Nothing could be easier. Allocate one large apple pie per man – you want some left over, don't you? Ask the best apple pie makers that you know to produce the pies. Buy in good quality cream and ice-cream. Print attractive invitation cards and distribute them to every man who has ever had even the slightest contact with your church.

This evening event is best held in a large house but the cleaned-up church hall can be an alternative venue. Make sure that all the play group toys are out of the way and all the soppy posters taken down. A by-product of the evening could be a group of men determined to redecorate and carpet the church hall.

Tea, good coffee and fresh orange juice should be available. There is no reason why the men should not look after them-selves. The pies can be served hot or cold (you do have a micro-wave, don't you?) and men can have small portions of several different ones and vote which one they thought was the best.

Christian conversation is an optional extra at this event but I doubt if you will manage to stop the non-church-going guests from turning the conversation around to religion sometime during the evening.

Background music for the evening can be a mixture of folk music and gospel songs.

You are building bridges with apple pies!

Local dish

In some areas of the country there is a specific local delicacy or dish. For example you will all know about Lancashire hot pot and Cornish pasties. If you live in either of those areas you have an excuse for another local culture food night for men.

Only serve the one course. This time you could include a brief presentation of another local fact, that of how Christianity first came to your area.

Ask your local librarian to help with the research and if a man, don't forget to invite him to the event.

In Bedfordshire, your research into local dishes would certainly uncover the Bedfordshire clanger. Yes, that really is the name. It was a kind of 'sweet-and-sour' cornish pasty. The Bedfordshire landworkers were paid for the amount of greens or potatoes that they bagged. Lunch was a luxury eaten at the edge of the field. They took a pasty which had meat at one end, or more usually just vegetables with a bit of meat gravy on them, then there was a partition barrier of pastry part way along and the other side was filled with jam or fruit.

So you started at one end with the savoury and ate your way through to the sweet. Not as good as Lancashire hot pot, but it does have huge publicity value if you do it in Bedfordshire.

Home dinner party

The third arena for a food invitation to men is the small

dinner party in a home. Here, you prayerfully choose which men to target and to invite. Make it a 50/50 mix of Christians and uncommitted men. Don't invite the controversial types. No one minds a discussion but we are not interested in arguments on this occasion. You reach those types of men best on a one to one basis. Invite those men whom you know are open to the Christian message or who are already on the way to faith.

The size of the home will limit the attendance, probably to ten or twelve. The food can be quite plain as long as it is good home cooking. It doesn't all have to be produced in the same kitchen. The best home setting may not be the home of the best steak and kidney pie maker.

Men's food tastes are generally very limited. Don't serve the trout: some men will have difficulty lifting out the bones and men are so easily embarrassed by things like that.

The meal can include an after dinner speaker or two. Their talks should be brief testimony times rather than a theological treatise. Concentrate on the man that Christ has made you rather than how sinful you were when you were the local dominoes champion in 1972.

Don't forget some background music; it covers any awkward silences. Let the other Christians be prepared to question the speakers and then let it simply turn into one to one conversations over coffee. The men whom you invite know what they are coming to and are grateful for the opportunity to listen in a small group setting of other men.

Don't be afraid if the Holy Spirit prompts you to push the man you are talking to towards a real personal commitment. If he doesn't feel ready he will soon pull the conversation back to the safety of the weather or the state of the local football team. If you don't move him on towards commitment, however, he won't find it so easy to steer things that way. If there is no challenge maybe he will go away with the idea that you are not all that committed yourselves.

Restaurant meal

The bigger version of the home dinner party (although the food is often not as good) is to hire one of your local restaurants for a men's meal. More men are prepared to accept an invitation to a meal than an invitation to a church service.

There is no need to hide the fact that the meal is a 'religious event' and that the after dinner speaker will be talking about the Christian faith and how it works out today.

Far from putting men off, that will attract even more and will result in their having thought seriously about the subject before they arrive on the night that the meal is held. Why not include the title of the talk on your invitation card?

'Is there life after birth?'

'Christianity can seriously affect your death.'

'How to live forever.'

Give it some thought and you'll come up with a brilliant title. Any experienced evangelist will be able to work your title into his presentation of the facts about Jesus Christ. There is no rule in the Bible which says that only lay people can be the after-dinner speakers. Many talented evangelists are in full-time Christian work: make use of their God-given gift.

You will need an experienced evangelist for such a high profile event. He doesn't need to be a household name in Christian circles. Even if he was, the non-Christians probably wouldn't have heard of him. Ideally your speaker needs to come from a similar peer group to your expected audience. I heard recently of a dinner for senior executive business men where the invited speaker was a rough diamond, street preacher. Now his enthusiasm was beyond question but his background and his presentation style did not get through to his audience. They didn't hear the message because of all the 'noise' he was making. They were more used to the board room and he worked as if he was still in the fish market.

I'm not saying that God cannot or does not use such a testimony. I do feel that it would have been more effectively used at a fish and chips supper in the church hall, rather than in the five star restaurant where it happened.

Look at the local restaurants and find the best one taking into account quality of food, table layout and price range. Find out which is their poor attendance night. Every place has one. Then negotiate with the manager or the owner to give you exclusive use if you bring double his normal number of customers.

Again, plan to have a 50/50 mix between Christians and fringe people. At the end of the after dinner speechmaking you want Christians to be available to turn to the uncommitted man next to them and take the conversation further. The guests actually expect this to happen. At any business presentation that he attends, the conversation afterwards is always linked to the subject that brought them together. So if you avoid talking about God, your guest will decide that you only came for the food.

You will have used wedding reception type place names to make sure that you have strategically placed your talkative and quiet Christians amid the visitors. We don't want an extra deacon's meeting going on at the bottom table, do we?

Your specially printed invitation cards/tickets need to be available five or six weeks before the event. There are sometimes valid reasons why your guest cannot attend. You will then have to approach your second choice man and it all takes time.

I have already said that you never get a second chance to make a first impression, so the welcome that men are given when they first arrive is very important. As a speaker at many of these events, I find that often the men I spoke to at the door are the ones who listened more carefully and are the ones who made a response at the end.

So have your speaker there early, along with the Christian man who has the best welcoming technique. Whilst not suggesting that you go to the expense of hiring an official toast master, I do recommend that someone acts as master of ceremonies. When the guests have all arrived and the restaurant kitchen is ready he can ask people to take their places at the meal table. Make sure that you have the after dinner speaker in the best place to be easily seen and heard.

When everyone has found their places, the master of ceremonies gives a brief welcome and asks the guest speaker to introduce his topic for the evening and to say grace.

Introducing the topic means three minutes at the most. The men are hungry, remember. But putting in that seed thought right at the start means that some of the conversations over the dinner table will get round to Christianity. The introduction also gives the speaker an opportunity to try out his voice and allows the audience to hear the sound of his voice. My technique, given away free with every copy of this book, is to include in my introduction a line like, 'There are other men here tonight who have a personal faith in Jesus Christ. Some of them are a bit shy, give them a nudge over the main course and ask them why they are so sure that they will never die.' That always puts the Christians on the spot and starts some good conversations.

After grace, the background music can be played again. Check out beforehand that the restaurant's normal taped music is not distracting. Don't replace it by gospel songs: words are a distraction on background music when you are trying to have a serious conversation. The next duty of the master of ceremonies is to gently interrupt when everyone has been served with coffee at the end of the meal.

He then deals with any commercials focusing on the next special event which will be of interest to the guests present. He does not go through a list of all the weekly church events or refer to the fact that next Sunday will be the pastor's forty second anniversary of coming to the church. He then, briefly and warmly, introduces the guest speaker and leads the applause.

It is always good to welcome the speaker with applause. It makes him feel great and makes the audience feel that he is better than he really is. It also gives the speaker time to stand up gracefully and to smile.

A good after dinner speaker may only talk for twelve minutes; or he may talk for forty minutes, but it only seems like twelve.

The after-dinner talk

Without sounding like a preacher, he will talk about and illustrate the relevance of the Christian faith for today's man, explaining how he can become Christ's/Man. He will present the basic facts about the Christian faith in a way that the fringe person can clearly understand.

At the end he should be able to offer a free copy of a suitable paperback book. You are thus demonstrating that the Christian faith is a serious and important matter for further thought. The speaker should offer the book to those who want to know exactly what is involved in becoming a modern day follower of Jesus Christ. Choose the book to match your audience.

When the evening finally comes to a close, the speaker should be strategically placed so that people can approach him; not entirely out of sight but not embarrassingly in the middle of the floor and under the spot light. The speaker should make a note of people's names, and possibly addresses, if they request a book. He promises to pray for them and indicates that someone else will make contact to see if they need any further help. It is essential that these follow-up calls are made within ten days; the leads go cold after that.

The speaker should also be prepared for personal counsel if it is clear that someone should be led to a point of decision there and then.

I have often felt it appropriate to end an after dinner talk with a simple prayer of response and commitment to God. The book is then offered to those 'who prayed the prayer and really meant it.' I have had the joy of seeing many genuine conversions at such evenings.

With or without a prayer – and the guest speaker must sense the guidance of the Holy Spirit in this matter – he should indicate that there are many others around the tables who can speak from personal experience about the reality of Jesus Christ. He should then invite people to have a second cup of coffee and to talk some more before leaving. This is the signal for the staff to serve more coffee and the after dinner mints, and for all the believers to take up any further opportunities to share their own faith and personal experience of God with their guests.

Who pays for it all? The Christians of course. An investment of around £10 per guest is not high in terms of God's investment in our salvation. Restaurants will usually provide a very reasonably priced set meal as long as the main course is the same and starters and sweets are restricted to a choice of two or three.

Meal with a meaning

A variation on the meal in a restaurant is to hold the much more exciting and nerve-wracking 'Meal with a Meaning' on church premises. Full details of how to arrange that are given in my book *An Evangelism Cookbook*. The £2.95 you pay for that book will be saved many times over as the practical advice given saves you from making costly mistakes.

Men's breakfast

I am often told that when some men get home from a hard day, slaving over a hot office desk, they don't want to do anything at all, not even to go out for dinner.

Saturday breakfast is often then the breakthrough point. Most men only have a cooked breakfast on holiday or on their birthday if that falls on a weekend.

So the offer of a cooked breakfast at 8:30am on a Saturday morning is an attractive proposition. The venue can again be a local restaurant or your revolutionised church premises. Eight thirty is not too early if you are inviting men with young families; babies and young children do not allow you to have a leisurely lie-in. An escape route for one Saturday morning, now and again, is, therefore, another plus factor.

If you make sure that the whole event ends at 10am PROMPT, then you are on a winner. The guarantee to his wife that he will be home by 10:30 ensures her co-operation and makes him secure in the knowledge that no one will be able to keep him locked up in church longer than he intends to be.

You don't need to serve cereal, porridge and orange juice as starters. The men have come for the bacon and eggs. A decent glass of orange juice will do him more good and get the saliva glands going as he smells the frying pans on the go. It also helps the digestion of the bacon fat. You could add toast and home made marmalade to go with the coffee and tea.

You may be able to make some kind of visual presentation of Christian facts using an overhead projector and screen during the breakfast; not talking them through, just displaying the visuals. If it can be done with humour or in cartoon style all the better. The after breakfast speaker acts like an after dinner one. Make sure you choose an evangelist who is at his best in the mornings; some of them are only programmed to come alive at seven o'clock in the evening.

Sunday fellowship lunch

Food and more food. Well you did ask for ideas so here's another one. A Sunday fellowship lunch. This time there is no speaker and no hard sell. It is a time to build contacts and let non-Christian men see that church people are touchingly human. Churches should be holding such lunches to build up the fellowship between each other at regular intervals anyway but don't miss the bridge-building opportunities that they also provide you with.

One lady told me that she couldn't come to the fellowship lunch because she would have to go home and make her husband his lunch. I suggested that instead of doing that she should give him the chance of coming to church for lunch. She did and he came. He was delighted to come to a church event where he knew exactly what he had to do. He knew how to eat.

Our practice has been that one person organises the other people to bring food. They found out what different people were good at and ordered some. All the food was set out on tables and everyone helped themselves. She simply said to her husband. 'Lunch is at church next week, we are all taking some food and sharing it out.' He described it as the feeding of the five thousand. But at the end he was impressed because everyone, including himself, had been well fed but there was nothing wasted and all these Christians were actually sane people. Some of them were even quite interesting to talk to.

He became a Christian himself about six months later.

BarbeQue

One last addition to the food approach to men has to be to organise a BarbeQue.

Here again we are bridge-building. I suggest that the event is seen as a family gathering and the fringe men are there to do the cooking. Nothing gives a man more of a sense of success than outdoor cooking. He only has to turn the beefburgers and the sausages over. That is after spending two hours getting the charcoal going properly. If he burns a sausage here or there that is called 'charcoal grilled' and they all taste good in the open air.

If you do anything by way of a Christian presentation at a BarbeQue event, make it visual; a short, colourful drama, a mime, a clown item, puppets. But get away from talk and more talk. The talk can come later when men are asking questions.

If you are near a seaside then it could be a beach BarbeQue, or down by the riverside, or on a farm or even on the church lawn. Don't worry about BarbeQue crashers (gate crashers): just welcome everyone and have fun.

That's a key factor for men. They have this fixed idea that Christianity is all about saying the right words in the right way in the right place. Show them that it's real fun to be a believer.

In Britain you run the risk of weather problems with outdoor events. Do you think that the global warming is improving our climate? My advice is to have the event ready for short notice presentation. All the food can be in the freezer. The weekly weather forecast will then enable you to give everyone forty eight hours warning. People who miss this one will come to the next. Get friendly with your area weather man: he may have always wanted to wear the chef's hat himself.

Do-it-yourself

One of the main growth industries in the United Kingdom in recent years has been in the number of large, out of town do-it-yourself stores. 'B & Q it' or 'Do-it-All': those are the slogans that man has heard and acted upon. Skill levels have varied and some men don't seem to have learnt much from their efforts, but many have tried. I have seen some very professional work in kitchen fitting carried out by a hospital porter and a beautifully built patio wall produced by a bank manager.

Both were supported by admiring wives. I suspect that both wives were quite convinced that their husbands would make a mess of it and were amazed by the end result.

If by getting involved in a do-it-yourself project, I can prove to myself that I am action man in person, impress my wife and save money at the same time, then man, I am for it.

The saving of money isn't very likely, at least in the early days, because I'm buying the right tools to do the job. At the end of several projects, I have a lot of tools although I haven't actually saved very much.

But at least I know that the item will stand the test of time. A wardrobe that I built in 1959 is still as good as new even though we have had to dismantle it every time we moved house. My wife says that is six times.

In a recent letter the Christian wife of an unconverted husband told me how thrilled she had been when, after four

years of witnessing to her husband, he had agreed to come
to church. Even better than that, he had agreed to come on
the church weekend houseparty. His coming meant that she
and the two children could also be there, for the first time.

Imagine her disappointment when, on arriving at the
Centre, her husband volunteered to look after the children
– their own and those belonging to the other families as well.
He didn't attend a single adult session held during the
weekend.

I am not at all surprised. He didn't have any idea what
would happen in the sessions; no one had explained them
to him, on the assumption that everyone knows. He did
know some of what was involved in looking after children
and organising sports for them, so he opted for the action
pack rather than the sedentary rows. He was adopting a
man's 'toe in the water' approach to Christianity: test it out
a little before you take the plunge.

What saddened me about the church involved, was that
they accepted his offer to look after the children but didn't
designate another Christian man to join him. In fact they
didn't give him any help at all; they just let him get on with it.

I am quite sure that the non-Christian husband came on
the weekend to hear about Christianity but he didn't yet want
to attend any meetings. If another Christian man had helped
him with the children there would have been many
opportunities to talk. Probably it would have been the non-
Christian who started the conversations about faith. He was
a do-it-yourself man.

An offer of help

A lady who plays the organ in a Sussex church has recently
had the joy of seeing her husband come to know the Lord
– but the church almost prevented it from happening.

The man was caretaker for a local school. He had always said that he was too busy to come to church on a Sunday. He felt the times were inconvenient and very often he was catching up with repair jobs on the school premises or acting as security guard to keep children from causing any more damage.

His wife played the organ most Sunday mornings and prayed for her husband for over thirty years. Retirement time came from the caretaking job and the husband was quite pleased to be relieved from the strain of it all. After years of watching the time they presented him with a clock to mark his retirement.

He began to run his wife to church on a Sunday morning and to collect her again at the end of service. Look out for the husbands who do that. They are trying to find a way in. You need to give them a do-it-yourself way.

The ex-caretaker commented one day to one of the church deacons, who was standing around waiting for his wife to finish talking as well, that the church window frames needed a bit of repair work doing to them. 'I'll give you a hand if you want,' he said, 'I've got time on my hands nowadays.' 'Thank you, I'll let you know,' said the deacon.

Non-Christian men, especially action types, do find it hard to understand why some things in church take so long to decide about. The husband kept asking his wife if anything had been decided and the windows got steadily worse. The church, meanwhile, had set up a sub committee (windows) to report to the main committee (buildings) to make a recommendation to the church diaconate, which would, in turn, include it on the church meeting agenda.

There was unease amongst one or two members. The offer of help had come from someone who wasn't a church member, not even an attender. Maybe he was trying to do his bit for the church and work his way to heaven. Now we couldn't allow that could we?

I am so glad that the minister had the courage to bang their heads together. He, at least, saw that this retired man was looking for a contact point that brought him into the church in his own right.

He didn't want to be the organist's husband. He didn't want to be brought to the services by his wife. He was a do-it-yourself man.

The minister gave up his own day off to help with the window repairs and learnt some new skills and gained some great illustrations in the process. It wasn't long before the retired caretaker was asking religious questions in such a refreshing and open way that the minister began to look forward to his practical day.

The ex-caretaker did come to a Sunday morning service about three months later, when all the windows had been finished. He was invited by the deacon who had talked to him in the beginning, to a special guest service with a visiting guest speaker. There was nothing unusual about the service; it was no different from normal except that the visiting speaker did have the gift of the evangelist. He put things into words that were right for the fringe person and he gave a clear opportunity at the end for people to make a personal response. One man was converted that morning – the man the church almost managed to keep out.

My observation is that working man, artisan man, understands more clearly by doing than in any other way. He can grasp things better with his hands than with his mind. How many workmen, I wonder, were converted as they constructed the great cathedrals of our land?

They were not word-based men but they saw the glory of God and worshipped the Master-Craftsman, the Creator of the universe. That can be the first step to Christian faith.

Practical work

It is a fact about men that they are not as good at words as
women. They are not as good at the small talk. That is why
you will often see the women talking to each other at the
end of a service and the men standing round on their own
just waiting.

If all of our church outreach is only based on words or books
or sitting in silent rows listening, then we will fail to reach
the do-it-yourself men. I am not saying that men will not listen
to a good speaker, but then how many of our speakers really
do grab an audience and take them on step by step?

I have met with churches where the only practical work
possible is to join the church cleaning rota or the twice a year
blitz on the euphemistically called 'garden'. Neither of those
are action man tasks. Unless cleaning means getting rid of
all the rubbish in the church and gardening means rotovating
and laying to lawn with the purchase of a sit-on mower to
cut the grass. Then you'll have the men all wanting to have
a drive on the mower.

One church had a local builder amongst its membership.
He did a whole series of practical demonstration evenings
for men, with some hands-on experience. The night they
did 'How to build a patio wall', fifteen men who had never
come before attended.

No doubt all of them wanted to impress their wives with
their building skills at some later stage.

Another area has to be that of basic car maintenance. Some
help for men on simple plumbing jobs and an understanding
of electrical circuits might come in useful. We tend to forget
that with modern housing and the hectic childhood in front
of the television, most men have never been tutored by their
dads in general household maintenance skills. It's quite
possible that their dad didn't know either.

Build the do-it-yourself bridge to men.

I wouldn't, in fact, limit man's desire for do-it-yourself just to the practical realm. I will talk in later chapters about other ways to reach men and some of the subjects that they want to cover. Issues of mental do-it-yourself are also recognised by men. How does the father keep up with his nine year old son once they have bought the computer for Christmas? If you offer some basic teaching times for fathers who have missed out on computers then you have a ready made audience amongst the over-forties.

Try it and you'll discover that I am right.

Sport and fitness

I do not have the figures to prove it but I do have a hunch that the majority of men in our churches are less sport orientated than the average man in the United Kingdom as a whole.

They are certainly not as physically fit as Mr Average but that could be accounted for by the number of times they sit through church meetings and the fact that they are always late for meetings and therefore have to go everywhere by car.

The reason for having less sports 'minded men in our churches than in the local population could be that our woman orientated message has attracted the men with the most feminine attitudes and characteristics. That would be compounded by the fact that we then draw those men deeply into the life of the church family and look down on any attempt that they might seem to make in continuing to reach the outside world of men.

Talk to any group of non-Christians and sport is guaranteed to come out as a topic of conversation. Perhaps again our Christian fervour seems somewhat muted when men are used to the evangelical zeal of the Cop End at Anfield in Liverpool.

Can we somehow restore the idea that to be a fit man and a Christian are not contradictory terms. Paul's words about 'bringing the body into subjection', and 'bodily exercise profits only a little', and 'I beat my body', do not imply that we should not be involved in any form of exercise programme.

Callisthenics for men has to be a winner for the 1990s. It is an exercise programme which doesn't involve you in too much leaping about. Just right for men. I visited a church which ran a very professional aerobics class for ladies, called, interestingly enough, 'Fitness for Life'. Over one hundred were on the books with a waiting list of ladies wanting to join. I asked why they couldn't run one for men as well. They told me that men were welcome and about three men actually attended. Can you imagine being one of only three men leaping about to pop music with a crowd of women?

Start an entirely separate group for the men, they are so shy.

Weight training

Try the weight training approach. Look at what all the executive business travel hotels are adding to their list of facilities. En suite bathrooms, colour TV and in-house videos are old hat nowadays. It is the jacuzzi, the sauna and the exercise gym which now find a place in all the latest developments. The business man at the end of the day wants fitness — at least some of them do.

You will find that a lot of the men who are on the edge of your church's sphere of contact have a yearning to have a go at pumping the weights. Very few of them will have tried. They are not so keen on the idea that they want to join a proper club, nor are they prepared to buy a home gym for themselves before trying it out somewhere. It is a real market opportunity for the church. Set up an exercise gym in the choir vestry. You don't have much use for that room nowadays.

Throw out all the old broken chairs that are stored there. Change the lighting and give the room a look of purposeful manliness. In other words get rid of the pink rose wallpaper.

Then borrow or hire some equipment, preferably with a qualified instructor for the night. The local sports shop may be able to get a company rep to come and demonstrate appropriate equipment, but expect this to be from the top end of the price range and be prepared for the evangelistic sales talk.

An alternative scheme is to hire an hour of time in the weights room at the local sports and leisure complex, or in a nearby hotel. You'll be surprised how many men want to come. Some men have not even had a go on an exercise bicycle. They do want to be able to try alongside other men who are also total novices. The men's group at church gives them exactly the right opportunity.

A church in Lancashire ran a very successful team marathon in their town. Teams of seven were invited from all the local pubs, clubs, schools and business firms. No team member could run more than five miles and all seven had to take part. Teams were allowed to raise sponsorship for a charity of their choice. An entry fee covered administration costs and prize money for individual winners in the men's and boy's categories. The whole event was hyped up by the local press and there was a huge turn out on the day. They even saw a creditable third place for the local church team.

A variation on that theme is a swimming marathon.

Local sponsorship

Why not advertise your church in the programme of the local town football team? In the junior leagues that isn't a costly venture and your name is being associated with a man's activity. Will it stop swearing on the field? I doubt it, but that doesn't rule out the idea altogether. A variation is that the church sponsor the man of the match award. That might only cost you £10 for a minute or more of advertising to all the men and their sons who are watching the game that day, plus the people outside the ground who hear all the loudspeaker announcements.

'Player of the match today is John Birtles of Lower Warrington FC. The award is sponsored by the Lightbourne Baptist Church. The Lightbourne Baptist Church, well, that might be worth a visit, match of the day there is at 10:30am, I believe.' You've made contact with the club chairman to offer the sponsorship and the club secretary to pay over the money in advance, and now you've impressed the commentator (who happens to be the local electrician), and the cub reporter from the local paper – and all for a few pounds.

Are you into squash? No, not a lot of young people in someone's front room and not a fruit drink, either. The sports version. The church could hire the local squash courts or badminton court or even the whole local leisure centre, and put on a Christian sports evening.

Could you arrange for a Christian sportsman to give a demonstration of skills, and over refreshments at the end tell the story of how he became a real Christian?

Could the fathers and sons go bowling? Try a 'Bring your dad night'. Try the crown green variety or the ten pin version. A single knock-out competition with a prize for the winner adds an extra dimension to the event. Or you could always arrange a sponsored parachute jump to buy medical equipment for the local ambulance or doctor's surgery. You might be the first to need it.

Once you begin to think along sporting lines then a whole lot of possibilities open up. I'll bet you have more ideas than you can use.

Again we have to say that some of the evenings and matches that you organise will do nothing more than make contacts and develop friendships and show you to be likeable, if unfit, specimens of manhood.

On other occasions you will be able to be much more definite about the claims of Christianity.

Food, do-it-yourself and sport can all be ways of winning men for Jesus Christ today.

Reaching the missing men

Here's a success story. A man in Scotland was converted two years ago. He had a background as a heavy drinker and his new found faith gave him the strength to give up and to stay off the bottle.

Within a month of becoming a Christian he asked the minister of the church if they could start up some kind of informal meeting for men, so that he could invite some of his old friends along to an event which wouldn't be as dour or as threatening as a church service.

The minister said that he would think about it and the leaders would discuss it. The months went by and despite repeated requests nothing happened. Most new Christians would have been crushed but this man had been so wonderfully delivered himself, he really did want others to have an opportunity to hear.

A year ago the minister was called to another church. The Christian with the burden for reaching men then went to the leadership and repeated his request for a man event.

They said that, 'Yes, there could be one, but there was no one to run it unless he did.' That usually finishes an idea but this man rose to the challenge. His first event was held in someone's home. He argued that men are more likely to come along to a home than to the church premises.

One of the church leaders was a fire prevention officer and so he was invited to talk about how to make homes safer and how to fit smoke detectors. There had been a tragic death of two children in a fire on the estate only a month before. The speaker also wove his testimony about salvation into his talk. Ten men attended: nine from the church and one total outsider.

The church men were disappointed, the ex-alcoholic was thrilled. A ten per cent non-Christian audience, to him, was a success.

The second event, about a month later, was a visit to a petro-chemical works some three miles out of town. William, the leader of the group, borrowed a piece of church notepaper and wrote to the managing director asking if a group of men from the church could visit the factory one Thursday evening. William didn't think to inform the deacons about the idea, he just took them at their word that he was to get on with things. The managing director, assuming that the letter was from the minister of the church, wrote back to say that his company would be delighted to entertain the men.

The firm would send a coach to collect them from the church. They would be given a works tour, shown a short film, provided with some refreshments and taken by coach back to town at the end.

Twenty-two men came to that event, nine from the church and thirteen outsiders. There were a lot of men who were curious about what went on inside that works, and if you are touring a workplace there won't be a sermon.

William, showing Christian maturity beyond his years, marshalled his nine Christian men and sat them one to a row on the bus so that the Christians had to talk to the non-Christians. There were some good conversations about the church on the way back.

His third event was to hire a copy of the video 'Hoddle' which gives the testimony of footballer Glen Hoddle, and to ask permission to show it on the large screen video at the local working men's club.

Realise the personal risk that he took in even going back on to licensed premises. William is determined to win men for Christ. As a result of the video the first outsider, who had come to the fire prevention night, has become a believer. One other man has started to attend church again and three of the local football team watched the Hoddle story. It was no coincidence that it was shown on practice night.

The story goes on as one man works at reaching the missing men. Even if other men in the church are not as keen as you are at the moment, that is no reason for delay. Why not start right now?

Action Page

Action proposed	Strategy outlined	Date fixed	Person responsible
Food			
Apple pie night			
Local dish night			
Home dinner party			
Meal with a meaning			
Restaurant meal			
Fish and chips night			
Men's breakfast			
Sunday fellowship lunch			
BarbeQue			
Another brilliant idea			
DIY			
Church renovation			
Chair mending			
Car projects			
Building a wall			
Plumbing			
Electrical			
Another brilliant idea			
Sport			
Callisthenics			
Weight training			
Team marathon			
Sponsored swim, walk			
Local football advert			
Squash			
Badminton			
Leisure centre night			
Bowling			
Parachute jump			
Another brilliant idea			

Chapter 9

Christianity is not for wimps

A new young minister in a Baptist church down in the south-west of England discovered that in his church he had ten women who had become Christians, whose husbands had no link with the church at all.

He immediately decided that he was going to do something about the situation in order to bring about a change.

Now many church leaders would have formed a committee which could have looked at the problem. They would then have read any books on the subject, and consulted with other churches which had a similar problem. They would obviously have attended any Christian conferences or Spring Harvest seminars about this matter and by the time that they had reported back, with any luck, that young minister would have moved on to another church and no one would have needed to do anything about the problem.

My young friend had not grown up in church circles. A fact which is obvious when I tell you that he didn't call together a committee. He never thought about such a tactic: he just wanted to see the men converted.

So he did the obvious thing and sent a letter to each one

of these uncommitted men asking them to come round to his home one Thursday evening for some food and to talk about why they were not yet committed to Christ when their wives had obviously made a real response of faith.

I consider him to be one of the bravest young men that I have met recently. Fancy inviting ten articulate, argumentative men into your home and taking them on single handed. In actual fact he wasn't single handed, because his church secretary heard about it and came along in support. It was still a bit like a tag wrestling match and they were outnumbered on the night eight to two.

If the minister had followed up his letter with a personal telephone call it would probably have been ten to two.

An open debate

The minister introduced the evening by telling a bit of his own story. He had come to faith later in life after quite a wild career and believed that God was real; if God could change his life, he could change the life of any man there as well.

He then opened the evening up for questions and they tore him to pieces. They asked him questions that he had never heard before. They told him exactly what was wrong with his church. They wiped the floor with him! Of course he managed to say one or two good things but, at the end, he felt a complete failure.

He was relieved when the time arrived to eat the food which his wife had prepared earlier and he closed the evening by saying that he would go away and think about some of the things that they had said. 'Give me a couple of weeks', he said, 'and I'll meet you again like this and give you some of the answers that you have asked for.'

The men enjoyed the food and were very friendly during

the coffee time. They congratulated him on how well he had done. They had all enjoyed it and about half of them said that they would certainly be coming again. One man asked about bringing his new baby to church, 'for one of your dedication things.' What completely floored the minister, however, was one man's request to become a believer there and then. 'Will you pray with me?' asked the man. The minister had earlier mentioned that he had become a real Christian after someone had prayed with him and had given him a prayer to say. No one seemed at all embarrassed.

So one husband, previously uncommitted, became a Christian that day. He had actually been waiting for an opportunity to make a start at following Jesus. He had noted the difference since his wife had become a believer and wanted to be in on the action.

How many other men are waiting for us to get out of our religious security zone and into the real world where they live?

Do you know much about the men who are on the fringe of your church life? Where do they work? What interests do they have? What activities do they attend if they don't come to you or do they actually spend every spare moment in front of the television?

Have you asked any of them to tell you what they think about God and the church and religious faith? You might discover that they have more sneaking admiration for fanatical Muslims rather than for dull Christians. At least the fundamentalist takes things seriously and shouts loudly about just what he believes, repeating the words often enough for you to get the message. The faith of some of these way-out people clearly affects their lives and life-styles. Maybe the outsider wants to know how much our faith affects us?

Are you willing to be challenged?

Have you tried to find out what your non-Christian men want to know about? What does interest them or spark off a lively conversation in the pub?

Let's take a few risks and take on the world with our faith. Let's meet some of these men, nose to nose, to hear what they have to say and to make sure that they have heard what we have to say.

The conclusion that I have reached from contact with a large number of churches in the United Kingdom is that we are afraid of such encounters in case we lose the argument.

The other reason for our fear is that we don't actually know what we each believe ourselves and so feel that we might be embarrassed if we have to defend a position that we don't hold. For example, only last month I was amazed when a Christian friend of mine came out with the suggestion that the world had been made in 4004 BC. He hadn't got that from the Bible at all, it was a quaint suggestion made by Archbishop Usher who was Anglican primate of Ireland in the seventeenth century. The dear Archbishop thought that he had managed to add up all the ages of all the people mentioned in the Old Testament part of the Bible.

Now I had to say that I didn't agree with my Christian friend. It didn't end our friendship but it did cause quite a stir.

Often in our churches we hide our differences about politics or the environment or any other real life issue for fear of disagreements. How can we ever take on the world outside if we haven't faced up to one another? I ought to be able to debate issues with you and maybe we will remain on different sides of the fence; but it should not threaten our oneness in the Spirit.

Christianity is not for wimps.

If we are to reach men with the Christian message then it is clear to me that we will have to talk about the questions which arise in our real world. We will need to relate our faith to the newspaper headlines of our day. We need to go for discussion. We need to train our minds to be Christian apologists and engage in Christian apologetics.

Spokesmen

I do not mean that we apologise about our faith, in fact, exactly the opposite. We go on the offensive. Here is one of those English words where people are confused about the real meaning.

Look up your dictionary definition of 'apology' and you will probably read, 'Regretful acknowledgement of fault or failure; assurance that no offence was intended; explanation, vindication.'

Now use your Concise Oxford Dictionary to look up the word apologist. It doesn't say 'one who apologises.' It actually says, 'One who defends (eg Christianity) by argument.' The word comes from the Greek source *apologizomai* – to render account.

I want Christian men to render an account of their faith to other men. It is time to give an account of ourselves.

I suppose that the very word 'Christian' has itself become devalued over the years. In its popular usage most people take it to be a description of anyone who is decent and civilised. Christian is the name that you generally give to anyone who doesn't openly avow to being a Buddhist or a Jew or an out-and-out atheist.

People get very offended in our country if you say that they are not Christians. They are decent, civilised people. Some of them even go along to church now and again.

I have been searching for a replacement word which

would stress the uniqueness of personal Christian faith. I think that I have found it in 'Christ's/Man'.

When we take a look at our own lives we do not usually see the flaws which stand out to those who know us well. We are too close to ourselves to see the bad things and too proud to admit the mistakes.

When we place ourselves alongside others we are usually wearing our best outward appearance and it is easy to say, 'I'm as good as they are!' or even, 'I'm better than that.'

In a so-called Christian country we, therefore, take it for granted that we are all Christians. We don't go back to the Bible to find out the original meaning of the word. If we did we would find that 'Christian' was a nickname given to those who were disciples of Jesus. Those who were seen to be personal followers of Jesus Christ were given the name 'Christian'.

That's quite a long way from today's use of the word where it is applied to people who clearly are not following the daily instructions of Jesus. They, themselves, would admit that they are not that involved.

A new name

So I want to leave the word 'Christian' in its common use, as someone who is nice and civilised and kind to animals and introduce a new word for the personal followers of Jesus. I want a new name for the man who is committed to Jesus Christ. Let's call him Christ's/Man.

We live in an amazing universe. In fact, it is just that: a uni-verse, not a multi-verse. However far our expert scientific friends probe into space, they find that it runs on the same lines; gravity and velocity still apply. The laws of physics still hold good. The inescapable conclusion is that there is only one creative mind at work in our universe.

There is one God, and only one, managing and holding together the universe that He has made.

Dr Irwin Moon, who used to head up the Moody Institute of Science in Chicago, said, 'Here's how to count the stars. Go to the seashore and count the grains of sand. Count all the grains of sand on all the seashores of the world and you will have the number of stars in all the galaxies.'

The Creator/God who made them all, also made our world as a centre for His attention and as the habitat for His masterpiece. Out of all that He made, nothing was more complex or involved more risk of failure than God's/Man.

People were placed on the earth to run the world according to God's design. Their successful control of the world would, it seems, have led to greater things in space. The risk element was high, because God had not created computers or robots, but men. God had placed within God's/Man a freedom to choose to love and obey. That very quality opened up the possibility of hatred. God's/Man knew the good, he enjoyed the good things that God had made. Soon he had the potential to know evil.

The temptation proved too much for the people on earth. Man in his stupidity tunes in to the wrong television channel and accepts the lies that were broadcast.

The message he hears sounds like one of freedom: 'Break your links with God and you will be free.' Well yes, he was free – to disobey. Free to run the world his own selfish way. Free to blow a hole in the ozone layer or burn the rain forests. Free to pollute the rivers and even the sea itself. Free to go to war. Free to create a refugee problem. Man was free, but he could only head in one direction; away from God and that meant a downward spiral.

Once God's/Man brakes his link with God he becomes simply 'man'. In no time at all man becomes twisted, distorted, sinful, sadistic and above all self-centred.

God made man out of the chaos and man, when he had broken off his link with God, remakes the chaos again.

God's response

The logical thing for God to have done, it seems to me, would have been to throw away planet earth and start with a new man on a new planet.

God had a better plan. A man who had acknowledged his failure without God and who had been restored to contact with God would be a better man than any new design.

Recycled man, man who was restored and renewed, reclaimed and redeemed, would not only have the capability of love but would be committed to love. So God enters human history as 'God/Man'.

Jesus Christ is the complete one. He is fully man, you can tell it by the way that He gets tired and falls asleep in the boat or is hungry enough to send His disciples shopping even when the shops are likely to be shut.

But within Jesus Christ, God and man fuse together. Jesus is the God/Man. Occasionally the glow of the glory shines through to His followers. The end is beyond question. Men who are out of touch with God are not going to tolerate this kind of light in their midst. It reveals all the darkness. They have to put it out of the world.

That is just what a unique alliance of political parties and religious factions managed to do. Or at least that is what they attempted to do. They certainly rearranged his place on earth and placed him on a cross. They definitely took a lifeless body down from the wood and placed it in a sealed rock tomb.

What they seemed to fail to understand was that the true God/Man would be indestructible. Just as the original God's/Man would have lived for ever if he had maintained his link to Creator/God.

Suddenly the God/Man is back again. Those who link their lives to Him are transformed. It isn't just a new idea that they have got hold of, or a new theory; it is a new life. It is nothing less than the flow of God's life and power which now enters believing man. There is only one way to describe him. We must call him Christ's/Man.

Going further

In our apologetic of the Christian faith we need to spell out the challenge. There are so many people around us who are nice people but they need to go further; they need to become Christ's/Man. There are some who are regular church-goers but it is obvious from their lack of dynamic that they have still to become Christ's/Man.

I will write in Chapter 15, in the final section, about just how to become Christ's/Man.

I want Christ's/Men to get into serious discussion with the men of our society to present the challenge of our faith.

My observation is that many men respond to a challenge. What about presenting the competition element of Christianity to men of our generation.

I heard Donald English tell the delightful story of attending an evening of wrestling in his home town. The main feature was a contest between Giant Haystacks, a disreputable brawling fighter who was known to disregard the rules, and Big Daddy, the clean-living, honest wrestler.

Donald English describes how the lights in the hall went down and a roll on the drums announced the entrance of Giant Haystacks. A single spotlight picked him out as he shuffled towards the ring. As he came the crowd booed loudly. He snarled back and swore at them. He kicked people out of his way, pushed the old ladies over and climbed into the ring.

The referee warned him about his behaviour and was rewarded for his trouble by being tied up in the ropes and arm chopped.

Suddenly all the lights were on. A fanfare of trumpets sounded out. A whole battery of spotlights picked out Big Daddy striding towards the ring. He waved his Union Jack top hat to the cheering crowd. He stopped to kiss the babies and to pat the old ladies on the head. Just before he climbed into the ring a little boy ran up to him for an autograph.

Once in the ring, Big Daddy took hold of Giant Haystacks by the hair and paraded him round before knocking him over with one massive bump. The referee was released and dusted down.

'I realised,' said Donald English, 'just what wrestling is all about. It is all about the contest between light and darkness, and it is the light which wins.'

Why don't we make our sermons and services as exciting as that! We need to challenge men to join us in the conflict.

The challenge of Jesus

Perhaps we ought to look again at the way in which Jesus Himself presented His Kingdom message to men. Immediately we notice the essential first fact. It was a Kingdom message. Jesus was not talking about some theory of religion to set alongside other theories. He was inviting men to get involved in a Kingdom.

Man has always wanted to be Action Man. That's why so many boxes of chocolates are sold to men to give to their wives or girl friends. In giving the box of chocolates men remember the classic television advert where the man dives off the cliff top into the sea. He swims through the shark infested waters, outwits the security system on the boat and enters the woman's locked cabin to place his box of chocolates on the bed. 'And all because the lady loves . . .'

Nonsense, it is all to do with man's desire for action, even if only in the world of fantasy!

It is time to drag our young men away from the fantasy games played on their computers and into the real conflict as Christ's/Man.

Jesus emphasised the Kingdom and also spelt out the cost of being a member:

Come follow me (Mark 1:16).

Without delay he called them (Mark 3:35).

Whoever does God's will is my brother (Matthew 7:29).

The secret of the kingdom of God has been given to you (Mark 4:11).

Whoever loses his life for me and for the gospel will save it (Mark 8:35).

Go into all the world and preach the good news to all creation (Mark 16:15).

The gospel records reveal many more incidents where Jesus, the supreme Action Man, calls men to action in our world. It is a message that needs to be heard more in our churches today.

We are still more likely to have a Bible study than to sign a petition. More often we set up a committee rather than hold a protest march. I am glad to see that Graham Kendrick's March for Jesus and the Evangelical Alliance's rediscovered stress on social action are beginning to move in the direction of Kingdom action and activity.

The Kingdom of God is for men who want to change the world. It involves having the courage to be changed oneself. Christianity is not for wimps.

Chapter 10

Man's standard arguments

In conversations with men there do seem to be a few arguments that crop up time and time again.

They are the defence mechanisms used by men when the challenge of Christianity begins to get a little too close.

I can remember visiting an engineering factory for a conducted tour. I have always been interested in what people manufacture and in this town, this particular company had a high reputation for the quality of its products. On arrival I was told that before I went round the workshops the Managing Director wanted to have a word with me.

His office was amazing. He was a clean desk man; a man who only believed in handling a piece of paper once, then it was either delegated or filed or put into the rubbish bin.

He came round from behind his empty desk to shake my hand 'Mr. Cook,' he said, 'so you've come to convert me.' 'No sir,' I replied, 'I've come to look round your factory, and anyway I couldn't convert you, God would have to do that.' I pointed heavenwards as I spoke.

I was invited to come back for coffee after my tour. When I returned, I met an agitated Managing Director. It seems that his wife had become one of these 'born-again Christians' about six weeks earlier. He was running scared. He had to acknowledge that what she had discovered had made a difference in her life. There was no doubt that the changes were for the better. But what would his colleagues say if he were to get converted?

So he took the line that you can't believe it, if you can't see it. 'That means that you can't possibly believe in God, can you?' he said. I disagreed.

How can you be sure?

There is an interesting response to the man who says, 'I know that no sensible person can believe in God.' When I used this argument years ago I used to say, 'No scientist believes in God; I just know that there is no God.'

Well, does anyone know the total truth in the entire universe? Of course not. Do you know even one per cent of all the truth that can be known in the universe? I've not met anyone who claims that figure. Once you have learnt anything, you realise how much more there is to learn.

How about knowing 0.1 per cent of all the truth in the entire universe? No, you don't know even that amount. Well even supposing for the sake of argument that you do know 0.1 per cent of the total truth in the entire universe, it is still possible that God is in the 99.9 per cent that you don't know and also in the 0.1 per cent that you do know – but you don't recognise him there.

It is therefore ridiculous to deny God's existence. You cannot disprove his existence. Ultimately it comes down to a simple question of faith. But then, that is true of all forms of knowledge.

David Watson, in one of his excellent books, talked about the three forms of human knowledge.

First there is mathematical or logical knowledge: the 2 + 2 = 4 kind of knowledge. The area of a triangle therefore is half the base times the height. So providing that I accept 'by faith' the basic principles of mathematics (and it is a matter of faith), I then gain new knowledge by sheer logical reasoning. QED – *quod erat demonstrandum*.

Second, there is scientific or experimental knowledge. Suppose I drop an apple and it falls to the ground. I keep on dropping apples and they keep on falling to the ground. Everyone does the same thing and every apple responds in the same way. I could then formulate a 'hypothesis' which I could call 'the law of gravity', except that someone else thought of it first. The hypothesis (a supposition made as a starting-point for further investigation from known facts) is then tested by further experiments. Then, providing that we accept 'by faith' the uniformity of nature (and it is an act of faith), I gain my new knowledge by further observation, hypothesis and experiment.

The third kind of knowledge is personal or experiential knowledge. This is quite different from the previous two forms of knowledge. In fact, when we try to express something that is intensely personal in scientific terms we get some hilarious statements.

You could say as a matter of simple observation that playing the violin is rubbing the entrails of a dead sheep with the hairs of dead horse. You would be describing the facts. But not all the facts! You would not be answering the question of why certain sounds are harmonious and others jar the senses. Why is music enjoyable at all? Or for that matter, why should the violinist be playing the violin?

Strictly speaking we may say that science answers the 'How?' questions but not the 'Why?' questions.

To take another example, a kiss is 'the approach of two pairs of lips with reciprocal transmission of microbes and carbon dioxide'. Next time you see a pretty girl and want to kiss her try saying, 'Let me give you a transmission of microbes and carbon dioxide'. See what her reaction turns out to be! Do remember to duck.

It is certainly not the most attractive way of expressing love.

David Watson asks, 'What is love? What is the beauty of a sunset? What is the spirit of a football team? These are real enough, but cannot be reduced to mathematical or scientific terms without making nonsense of the realities.'

The nature of proof

We can never really prove a person's existence unless we relate to that person. The only reality of knowledge is brought about by relationship.

When we talk about the existence of God, everyone exhibits faith. The atheist has faith – faith, in his case, that God does not exist. He has no proof. He is an atheist 'by faith'.

When we talk about faith in Jesus Christ we are not talking about some kind of blind faith. There is enough evidence to be seen which gives credence to the reality of God and to the inalienable facts of Christian truth. The accurate scientist does not claim absolute proof for some position but accepts something as true if the evidence strongly supports it. So the Christian believes that there is strong evidence to support his knowledge of God.

There is the evidence of the universe.

The heavens declare the glory of God;
the skies proclaim the work of his hands (Psalm 19:1).

There is the handiwork of beauty. 'I am looking now at a

red rose.' As a scientist I have evidence for that statement. But suppose I say, 'I am looking at a beautiful rose.' That statement cannot be tested in a colour laboratory but it is equally and maybe more powerfully true than my first observation.

We are accustomed to saying that 'seeing is believing', but there is a real sense in which 'believing is seeing'. Belief in God is not an act of blind trust with no rational basis.

Faith is, of course, needed, but then faith is needed for everything. Christian faith is much more than an intellectual assent to some proposition about God. Christian faith is personal commitment to the ways and purposes of God. The experience of commitment to God opens the way to a wider scope of insight than a merely intellectual seeker can ever know.

Life waits for this kind of venture of faith. It certainly opened my eyes.

But then, say many men, 'it doesn't matter what you believe, as long as you are sincere.'

What an amazing statement. In so many spheres it so obviously does matter what you believe and if you don't believe the right thing then you are wrong. If you play tennis you can sincerely believe that if the ball lands anywhere in the total court then it counts as in play – but that is only if you are playing doubles. In singles the court is narrower, and the line that counts is the inner line.

Millions once sincerely believed that the earth was flat and that if you sailed too far into the horizon you would fall off the edge. They were all wrong. Sincerity can't make wrong facts right.

However hard you think, you cannot come up with a real everyday example which supports the theory that all you need is sincerity. The world isn't made that way. The physical world is governed by laws of motion and gravity.

However sincerely you believe that you can fly, if you jump unaided off the top of St Paul's Cathedral in London you will kill yourself, whatever your religion happens to be.

Sincere but not right

My daughter is grown up now and works for a major company as an engineer building power stations. But she nearly didn't get to university. In fact, she nearly didn't get to school.

Her older brother had already started at school and it was the summer holiday time. We had booked a holiday in a delightful country cottage miles from anywhere. Just before the end of term there was an outbreak of measles in the school. Geoffrey went down with it and our holiday looked to be ended before it began.

Our doctor, however, said that Geoffrey had only got a mild attack and provided that we took certain precautions there was no reason why we should stay at home. So away we went.

As the doctor had predicted, Geoffrey soon recovered. Then young Helen fell ill. We were young parents but the obvious thought was that Geoffrey, always generous by nature, had passed the measles on to his sister. As that day progressed Helen grew worse. During the evening she showed signs of real distress.

I became so worried that I drove along the country lanes until I found a telephone box. I looked down the list of names and telephoned the first name listed 'doctor'.

It was a lady. She could have been a doctor of anything but by a happy coincidence she was a doctor of medicine and had a practice a few miles away. I described the symptoms and she came out straight away, arriving at our cottage near to midnight.

Her presence brought reassurance. She didn't feel that it was necessary to take Helen to hospital. She gave her some junior aspirin and we were told to give her some more if she woke in the night. The doctor would be back at eight in the morning.

I didn't sleep deeply that night and at about four in the morning heard Helen spluttering. I went in to settle her down, and crushed up the tablet from the foil wrapping and mixed it with a little baby food to get Helen to accept it.

She did because she was such a trusting little thing. Half an hour later she was violently sick. Just as well, because when we examined the wrapper, we found to our horror that I had given her one of my wife's asthma tablets, not a junior aspirin.

Don't ask me how one of those tablets got mixed up with the junior aspirin. I don't know. I was clearly sincere in wanting to help the child, but I almost killed her because I was sincerely wrong.

The eternal world is also governed by laws of rightness and justice. They apply however sincerely we ignore them. When you get some things wrong it can lead to disaster.

When it comes to the facts of Christianity what we need is not a sincere view of God but an accurate one.

All roads lead to heaven?

'But don't all roads lead to heaven?' I still meet people who know nothing about the facts of the world's religions who have made the dangerous assumption that different religions are just different ways to reach the same destination.

That is a non starter. How could it be so when so many different things are believed; some of them being the exact opposite of another religion's belief. There are religions which believe that their god is pleased with sacrifices, even human sacrifices. Others believe that their god is appalled by such an act. The two are clearly not worshipping the same God.

Hinduism believes in a multitude of gods. Islam is categorical in the fact that there is only one god. Buddhism doesn't give any clear answer about the nature or even the existence of God. Judaism describes His character in careful detail through the things that He has done.

Then what about salvation and eternity? In Hinduism it is the careful fulfilment of family duty. Ceremonial observances and self-discipline lead to salvation. Muslims, too, must fast and pray and recite their creed. Even then they are not certain to be accepted.

Christianity, alone amongst all world faiths, says that salvation cannot be earned at all; you can only receive it as the gift of God. The God/Man came to tell us that.

The world's great religions are certainly not going in the same direction or heading for the same destination. All religions do not lead to the same point any more than all the aeroplanes taking off from Manchester airport go to New York.

Why suffering?

'If there is a God, then why do so many innocent people suffer?'

For some men, sometimes this seemingly unanswerable question means in practice, 'Why hasn't everything worked out for me in the way that I wanted things to work out?' God is not into giving *carte blanche* answers to selfish prayers.

Let's examine the issue from an unselfish perspective.

C S Lewis, before he became a Christian, raged against

God because his own sense of kindness and justice was offended by much of what he saw in human society. He argued that a good God could not preside over such a world. Then C S Lewis began to wonder at the source of his own concern for love and justice.

Years later, after he became a Christian, he wrote:

My argument against God was that the universe seemed so cruel and unjust. But how had I got this idea of just and unjust? A man does not call a line crooked unless he has some idea of a straight line. What was I comparing this universe with when I called it unjust?

C S Lewis came to the conclusion that the only reasonable explanation for his own sense of injustice was a God of justice.

Does part of the answer to the problem of suffering lie in the fact that our time scale and God's plan are not in syncromesh? We want things to be sorted out now. Maybe the time will come when they are sorted out and everyone will see that even pain had a purpose.

Of course pain does have a purpose, as any doctor will tell you. It is the body's early warning system. If God were to remove pain completely it would be disastrous for the human race. It would mean that a hand could be burnt and we wouldn't realise soon enough to pull it away from the fire. When you go to a doctor with a pain, his first question is to ask where the pain is most severe because this helps him locate the problem and produce a diagnosis and a cure. Without pain, he would have a much more difficult job. Pain can be a friend as well as an enemy.

Then we must notice that suffering was never part of God's original creation. At the end of the account of God at work in Genesis chapter 1 we read,

God saw all that he had made, and it was very good (Genesis 1:31).

You only have to look around our present world to see that it is not as God intended it to be and it is clearly not God's fault. Man's greed and stupidity have crashed the gears of creation until, in the words of St Paul,

The whole of creation itself needs to be liberated from its bondage to decay (Romans 8:21).

The Bible seems to indicate that it was man's rebellion against God's order that resulted in a world in which struggle, pain and toil then became realities.

Cursed is the ground because of you; through painful toil you will eat of it all the days of your life (Genesis 3:17).

It is obvious that we are living in a creation that is spoilt and corrupted. Man was given control over the rest of creation so, when man went wrong, the inevitable consequence was that creation also went wrong. Much of our human misery is man made, not God caused.

Freedom is one of our greatest blessings, but it is also beset with great peril. God allows men to make their own choices, but by that decision He also allows us to reap the harvest of our own choices.

The greed of men

Even some of the natural disasters like earthquakes and floods have caused far more suffering and loss of life than was necessary, simply because of the stupidity or greed of men.

Years ago, a designer friend of mine was asked to produce

simple housing which could withstand earth tremors or which would minimise loss of life in major earthquakes. A few of his buildings were erected in various areas and in the years since, they have stood the test of time. Disaster has been averted. Many other areas have seen great tragedies in times of earthquake. It isn't that the expertise doesn't exist to build better, safer buildings. It is the will to spend the extra money on such buildings that has not been politically present.

Do you remember how many thousands suffered and died in the Ethiopian famine of 1985? Perhaps you also remember that more than two years before it all happened, relief organisations had warned governments that the disaster was on its way.

There was time to act. They could have ended the war. The government in Ethiopia spent millions, at the time, building lavish premises in Addis Ababa when, less than two hundred miles away people starved to death. You can't really blame God for all of that.

As far as Ethiopia is concerned, some would argue that European exploitation of the African continent is also at the root of the poverty there today. It was Mussolini who used the clearance of forests in that area as a means of giving work to unemployed Italians who started the desert, and that was in the 1930s.

As long as there is freedom of choice for man, some men will choose to cause suffering.

Then why doesn't God get rid of all the bad men in our world? If He did, would you be left?

Is there not within all of us an evil streak? Can any of us say that we have always done the right thing or said the best thing or thought the highest thing, all the time?

If not, then there is some evil within us. So if God were to get rid of all the evil, you and I would go as well.

A greater plan?

What if there is some greater plan than our minds can comprehend? What if time is only an incidental in it all? What if God has chosen a day on which all things will be made clear and when all wrongs will be put right?

If there is some climactic judgement day to come, then maybe the suffering of this world is put into perspective. That, in fact, is what Jesus taught. In many of His parables He indicated that there would be a final judgement day. On that day those weeds which have caused the suffering are ultimately removed and the good grain is harvested.

Let both grow together until the harvest. At that time I will tell the harvesters: first collect the weeds and tie them in bundles to be burned; then gather the wheat and bring it into my barn (Matthew 13:30).

What about the hypocrisy?

Men tend to have one more frequent problem about the Christian faith and this is a difficult one to answer:

'There are just too many hypocrites in the church.'

I think it is Charlie Brown of Peanuts fame who says, 'Society is great. It's just people I can't stand.'

Why should we expect all the people in church to be perfect? We don't expect that of any other group. Solicitors run off with their clients' money but it never gets the same press coverage in the popular press as when a minister runs off with the collection. By the way, I still go to a solicitor when I want a legal matter dealt with. I don't write them all off because of the actions of a few.

A popular definition of hypocrisy is, 'to say one thing and do another'. All of us are guilty of that from time to time.

Even the man who never went to church in his life but who leaves instructions in his will about the hymns to be sung at his funeral must be classed as a hypocrite. The church doesn't have a monopoly on hypocrisy, by any means.

If the accusation is that many Christians fail to live up to the high standards of the faith then that is probably correct. Each generation only produces a handful of saints like Mother Teresa. Is it such a bad thing to have tried and failed? Indeed, when Christians do fail they are usually harder on themselves than anyone else.

The Bible has a lovely verse about failure. It says,

If we claim to be without sin, we deceive ourselves and the truth is not in us. If we confess our sins, he is faithful and just and will forgive us our sins and purify us from all unrighteousness (1 John 1:8–9).

Now this is not a let-out for those who never try to live life at its highest. It is a constant reminder that, as we climb higher, we will trip up now and again. The way to continue is to get up and to go on with God. God knows that none of us is going to be perfect on this side of heaven.

It isn't very sensible to write off the whole of Christianity because we can spot a few defects in those who are trying to imitate Christ. Take a look at the original. He, the God/Man, Jesus Christ is magnificent.

As Stephen Gaukroger observes, 'Power failures don't discredit electricity; car breakdowns don't mean we never drive again. In both these cases, the principle remains valid even when an expression of the principle fails. If anyone doubted the existence or usefulness of electricity just because they have an old radio that doesn't work, we would doubt their sanity; yet people come to precisely this conclusion about Christianity on the basis of power failure among some Christians. There is absolutely nothing wrong with their power supply, they just seem to have faulty connections.'

Put it to the test

Why not put the matter to the test? You are honest enough to recognise that there is a lot of genuine faith amongst Christians. They may not have got their act completely together but they are performing better than most sections of society.

The claims that Jesus Christ makes are earth-shattering. He says that those who follow him are not left on their own to try to be good. He says that they are given a helper. One who will be alongside them. One who will actually live within their lives.

That's what we all need. We need the presence of God to enter our lives to make us into men again. We may sometimes hinder the working of that power or even quench His presence, but even then we are still better than we would have been if we had gone our own way.

When we get it all together with God then there is no stopping us. The sky is the limit. Let's go for the real thing. Let's be God's men again on earth.

I want to be a Christ's/Man.

Our next section is going to take a serious look at the differences that Jesus Christ makes in the life of a man who is really committed.

Section Three

The Christ's/Man in today's world

Chapter 11

Restored in the home

Towards the end of the 1980s a lot was said and written about 'the new man'. Magazines like *Cosmopolitan* and *She* carried questionnaires for their mainly feminine readership on what they would like men to become.

Surveys and research all came to fairly similar conclusions: they wanted a caring man. The new man would involve himself more with the family and the home.

House prices in some areas mean that both parents need to work in order to pay the mortgage, even after the arrival of children. The working wives want a man who shares in the work needed in the home.

In one survey in the South of England 62 per cent of the women were holding down full time jobs but they still had to do most of the housework. Only 5 per cent of men volunteered to do the shopping, 2 per cent the cleaning or washing and 6 per cent the ironing.

If asked specifically to help, then some 50 per cent of the men would help their partner with the shopping, but only 16 per cent would do any washing or ironing.

But it wasn't the household chores which came highest on the request list. Most of all, women want an understanding and a caring man.

There is a magazine for the new man called *GQ*, short for Gentleman's Quarterly. It has proved so successful that it is now published monthly.

A lot of the advertisements show smart, well dressed young men giving their baby a kiss or tucking their daughter or step-daughter up in bed. Whether these adverts are intended for the men or aiming to sell products to the woman is somewhat unclear.

GQ aims to present the image of a man who is strong enough to have 'feminine' characteristics. His caring and sharing in the home is all part of his father/mother image. For the first time, it is claimed, man can show the 'feminine' side of his nature. His 'motherhood' qualities can be revealed and admired.

It is all a dream. Man is not made that way. He does not have the biological functions nor the mind-set to make such an illusion come true. Media hype cannot change the way that man has been made. Recent articles in the *Sunday Times* magazine have reluctantly admitted that 'The New Man' hasn't appeared as some had hoped.

The differences again

In Section Two of this book I sought to show that there were fundamental structural differences between man and woman in the way that they would approach any issue.

Face a man with a crying baby and his logical brain process will diagnose trouble at one end or another! It needs food or a nappy change. If neither of these work he is at a total loss on how to deal with the situation. Women, not just the mother, pick up all the signals and process them through their intuition. They know that the baby just wants a cuddle. It wants some company, someone to play with.

To dream of a new man is a day dream. No doubt there

will be men who try to aspire to the new ideal and women who will only marry that kind of dream. It will take a few years before all the magazines are talking about the failure of the new man to be all that he promised to be.

Is it possible, however, to have a 'new born man'? Is a Christian man significantly different from an unconverted man? Is true Christ's/Man the ideal? Is woman's search for a new man a desire to have man as man was originally planned to be on earth? Would Adam, before his rebellion against God and Jesus Christ, fulfil all the criteria of new man?

And although in this life the image is never fully restored, could 'newborn man' be the nearest that any woman is going to get to the ideal? I believe that Christ's/Man is that ideal.

Because this is so, we need a major evangelistic outreach programme to men outside the church alongside a major teaching and training programme for the men who are already in the church.

What does it mean to be a Christian man? Just how wonderful is Christ's/Man?

We have a whole library filled with examples of God's men on earth. Not all are ideal examples. The failures are spelt out as well as the successes but – the plan of God, for man on earth, is there in the Bible to be studied and copied.

The power within

But not only do we have a blueprint and role models in the Bible; we have the aid of God Himself in becoming man as man was intended to be.

Jesus talked very little about the Holy Spirit until it got near to the time for Him to return to the Father in heaven.

Then Jesus taught the men who had begun to follow Him that they would not be left alone here in this world; they would have the help of the Holy Spirit. The Spirit would be their strength and their guide.

Look at the promises of John chapter fourteen. In verse sixteen believers are promised a Counsellor who will live within them, a guide into all truth. The words are repeated in chapter sixteen.

In verse twenty six they are promised a 'tutor' who will teach and remind them of the information that they need; a vital role, given man's brain structure. In verse twenty six of chapter fifteen they are promised an empowering so that they can talk about the truth of God. Remember, man isn't very good at all at words.

In verse thirteen of chapter sixteen they are promised guidance concerning the future so that they can lead others just as they themselves are led by the Counsellor.

So the Holy Spirit is going to do a restoration job on men. He is on the inside in order to sort out the failure of the past and so that He, the Counsellor, can guide man into the future.

Truth, memory, the ability to communicate and the power to lead are all promised to the newborn man. Perhaps it is time to leave aside our studies into who wrote the book of Hebrews and gather the men of our church together to train them in how to be God's man on earth today.

Perhaps if we made a real attempt at this we would produce, or rather God would have a chance to produce, a group of men who would attract the non-Christian man.

We might even merit some media attention for being nearer to the new man ideal than anyone else has managed to get by their own human effort.

Dealing with the past

For all men, even those who became Christians in teenage years, there are parts of the mind which contain facts and failures from the past. From time to time they re-emerge to cause pain or even chaos.

If we push wrong things down into the subconscious there is always the danger of a trigger device setting off an explosion. Then it all comes bursting out, sometimes as a breakdown experience.

The practical reality of Christian conversion is that God takes those sins and casts them away, *as far as the east is from the west* (Psalm 103:12).

They are cast *behind God's back* (Isaiah 38:17).

They are cast 'into the depths of the sea' (Micah 7:19).

Men need to remind themselves of these facts. As they walk in the light of God's word they are enabled to bring the darkness and its residual ashes out into the light which dispels it. The wind of the Spirit blows the chaff away.

As rebels against God, the evil one tricked us into programming our minds towards darkness. We thought and thought about owning that object until greed was fixed in our mind and, once stimulated, played the same tune over and over again. The object may have been a new car for the family or a new machine for the workplace now that we are self-employed. The result was always the same, a groove of greed etched into our memory pattern. We thought and thought about that person until the pattern of lust was fixed in our mind. The person became another object because man's mind is more able to handle objects.

After conversion, when we settle down to try and pray or read the Bible, we find unwelcome thoughts distracting our devotions. Material objects or people objects are used to draw us away from the security of forgiveness.

I believe that we need to teach men how to be free. It involves truth and memory. An assertion of the truth of God that *if the Son sets you free, you will be free indeed* (John 8:36).

This means that there can be a cleansing of the memory patterns which held power when you lived in the Kingdom of darkness.

The Holy Spirit alone has the ability to erase or disconnect the circuitry of evil which has been dominant in men's minds. The failure areas are different in different men although they usually cover money, sex and self-image. Maybe we need the brain washing which the Holy Spirit can give. We remember the truth. We are newborn men. We are forgiven men. We are free men. 'God has said it, I believe it, that settles it,' as Billy Graham says.

Then, when any mind circuit is encountered in practice we counteract it by pouring light into that area of darkness.

In Philippians, Paul talks about being a gentleman, a man as God intended:

Let your gentleness be evident to all (Philippians 4:5).

It is the picture of the newborn man. Then Paul writes,

Finally, brothers, whatever is true, whatever is noble, whatever is right, whatever is pure, whatever is lovely, whatever is admirable — if anything is excellent or praiseworthy — think about such things (Philippians 4:8).

Seven guidelines for godly thinking, because once a man's mind is reset on God then the man is at peace. He is a man of power to run God's world in God's way.

A new mind

We need to teach our men how to reprogramme their minds.

It must begin with truth. 'What is truth?' asked Pilate, because he also lived in an age of change when, if it was generally acceptable, then it must be allowable. There was no fixed point by which to measure man. Jesus Christ demonstrates that there is a reference point. Man must be measured against the God/Man, against the truth of what God intended man to be like.

Many things in our world are deceptive and illusory. They promise something which they never deliver. Wealth is like that. If only I had a little more but more only wants more. Parkinson's law applies that outgoings quickly rise to overtake any increase in income. Pornography is like that. The fresh government enquiry into whether violence in society is linked to hard core sex will discover how frustrated man becomes with the paper images. The moment arrives when he wonders if doing it for real will bring the thrill which he desires. Even when that is tried it is still unfulfilling.

Power is like that. Men who rise to positions of authority discover that the exercise of power, whilst flattering in its outward manifestations, is strangely empty at the heart.

Read what Charles Colson has to say about being at the centre of power in his book *Born Again*.

King Solomon said it all some three thousand years ago in the Bible book of Ecclesiastes. Over thirty times he declares that everything is meaningless. Nothing delivers the goods except truth. The mind that is fixed on truth discovers meaning and reality. A man who sets his mind on truth can rely on that which truth promises.

Set your mind on *aletheia*, that is the Greek word for 'truth'. Not merely truth as spoken but truth of idea and reality. Paul implies that fixing our mind on the centre of truth will result in us speaking truth, doing truth and maintaining truth. Our minds must be fixed on God.

This is eternal life: that they may know you, the only true God, and Jesus Christ, whom you have sent. (John 17:3).

I am the way and the truth and the life (John 14:6).

Learn by doing

How can you know the truth? by following the way. A man wrote to me recently saying that he wanted to know if there was a God. But he found that there were so many views around concerning Jesus Christ that he didn't know where to start. My advice was just to start. If he is genuine then God will graciously reveal himself. It is a valid scientific experiment; if you really want to know truth then seek for God. He has said quite clearly,

You will seek me and find me when you seek me with all your heart (Jeremiah 29:13).

If you hold to my teaching, you are really my disciples. Then you will know the truth, and the truth will set you free (John 8:31).

We need to declare that man can know truth. That declaration needs to start within our fellowship of men. Our newborn men must stand out as men of truth. Paul in Philippians tells us to set our minds on 'noble' things. The Greek word *semnos* literally means 'grave and worthy of respect'. It was the word which was characteristically used of the gods and the temples of the gods.

When it is used to describe a man it describes a person who moves through the world as if the whole world were a temple of God. It describes that which has the dignity of holiness upon it.

We set our minds upon God first of all, and that truth immediately reveals that man is made in the image of God.

Newborn man is, *God's temple (1 Corinthians 3:16).*

The liberating truth, once we have fixed our mind on God,is that we can think about ourselves. Man is then released into his full potential.

We can fix our minds on that which is right (see Philippians 4:8). The word *dikaios* means especially 'to be right with God'. Justices, in the sense that justice has been done and has been seen to be done in the heavens. I am righteous in the sight of God. I am not boasting about what I have done but I can boast about my Lord and His work of redemption in me. Do you see what this means? It means that newborn man is given the status that he has searched for and longed to possess.

Newborn man can walk tall, and as God's man on earth he can take upon himself the creation role to *fill the earth and subdue it . . . rule over it all* (Genesis 1:28).

Because of the work of Jesus Christ, man moves out of the curse of darkness into the blessing of God's light. So few men realise what becoming a Christian means! Even within the church the message is muted. Jesus told us to shout it from the roof tops. Newborn man is the temple of God, ruling and judging the world!

A new direction

Now Paul indicates in Philippians chapter four a new direction for our mind set.

Our minds are fixed on purity. The Greek word *hagnos* was the ceremonial word for that which had been so cleansed that it was fit to be brought into the presence of

God and used in the service of God. The implication here is that the Spirit of God, the Holy Spirit, can bring holiness into our minds. So much of the past has been sordid and soiled and shabby; the work of God in newborn man is to heal the mind with the sunshine of love.

It leads to loveliness. The word in Greek is *prosphiles* it might be paraphrased as, 'that which calls forth love.' Attractive and winsome qualities develop in the man who sets his mind on the love of God. Love seeps into every corner of his mind and affects his affections. So for wife and family, friend and neighbour there is a new ability to love in newborn man.

There are men whose minds are so set on vengeance and punishment that they call forth bitterness and fear in others. There are those in our world whose minds are so set on criticism and rebuke that they call forth resentment in others. The mind of the Christian man is set on the lovely things and the love of God flows through him.

What about the admirable things? These are actions of grace which can be made real by the man of God. The word *euphema* is linked to good harvests. As Jesus once said,

Some seed fell on good soil. It came up, grew and produced a crop, multiplying thirty, sixty or even a hundred times (Mark 4:8).

The word had a special connotation. It was used in ancient religious ceremonies to describe the holy silence at the beginning of a sacrifice in the presence of the gods. It was the words of prayer said in the heart in the quietness before God.

There are ugly words and false words, corrupting words and impure words. They bombard us from every angle and enter our homes via the miracle of radio, television and satellite.

Newborn man has an antidote to evil words. He is enabled to speak words from the Lord.

The pursuit of excellence

Finally Paul uses a word which was well known in classical and Hellenistic Greek, but does not appear elsewhere in Paul's writings, and only twice more in the New Testament (1 Peter 2:9 and 2 Peter 1:3). The word is *arete*. In classical thought it described every kind of excellence. It would describe the excellence of a pasture field the excellence of a craftsman's tool, the physical excellence of an animal which had taken the pride of the show place, the excellence of the courage of a soldier in battle. The word *arete* stood for everything which the secular world praised.

So Paul states the fact that Christian man has the ability to attain and surpass all that this world aspires towards. At its best, this world cannot reach the heights of which Christian man is capable. The world's longing for a new man is transcended in every area by newborn man. Newborn man is the one who knows truth because he has found God. That discovery has made man aware that he is God's temple on earth, set free from darkness and given the status of a son of God.

These truths release him to purity in his thoughts, love in his actions and honour in his words. It is all so much higher than secular man can reach. It is all the work of the grace of God.

We programme our brains. It is possible for newborn man to reprogramme his thinking and replace the old thought patterns of evil with new patterns of truth. The practical outworking of all of this meets its challenge in the home and in the marriage relationship.

Remember that the Holy Spirit is given to man to enable him to express all the truths concerning Jesus Christ.

And you also must testify (John 15:27).

Go into all the world and preach the good news to all creation (Mark 16:15).

You will receive power when the Holy Spirit comes on you, and you will be my witnesses (Acts 1:8).

The crowd on the day of Pentecost were amazed that they heard these men 'declaring the wonders of God'. It was the fact of declaration which proved an even greater miracle than the many tongues used.

The early disciples realised that they had to constantly pray for the power to *speak your word* (Acts 4:29).

And Paul asked for the church's prayers, *that I may proclaim it clearly* (Colossians 4:4).

Now the message of Christ concerns the love of God. It is a message that all who repent and believe may receive the riches of God's grace.

The Holy Spirit gives to man the ability to declare the truth of God. Man's difficulty with words is overcome by the enabling power of the Holy Spirit, and newborn man is able to speak of love.

Impact on marriage

It is not a coincidence that Paul uses this ability to speak of love when he comes to talk about the marriage relationship between believers. Christian men are to be

imitators of God and . . . live a life of love (Ephesians 5:1-2).

Where is this love to be demonstrated? In newborn man's love for his wife:

Husbands, love your wives . . . Husbands ought to love their wives as their own bodies (Ephesians 5:25, 28).

Ask any wife what she most wants and she will say that she wants her husband to tell her that he loves her. It is in this area of verbalising the message of love that man so often fails; man 'says it with flowers' or with a box of chocolates. But she wants to hear it in words. It is the God-given gift to newborn man that he has a Holy Spirit ability to talk about love.

That same Holy Spirit then leads newborn man into the position of leadership in the home.

Again, in my experience, many women wish that their husbands would be stronger and clearer leaders.

It is part of God's plan of restoration to give back to man the task of leadership in the home. Both husband and wife submit to Christ and in the task of priesthood within the home the wife submits to and respects her husband.

The challenge to newborn man is to accept the task of being spiritual head of the household. When this headship is claimed and exercised, women are truly liberated to be themselves and children have a balanced model of the fatherhood of God at the heart of their family life.

The United Kingdom is moving towards a situation where the only families remaining together could be those who have the power of the Holy Spirit and who live according to the role model of the Scriptures. To take headship involves more love from both partners, not less. To be head of the household means that our wives and children are due more love, consideration and care, not less.

The power to lead, the power to take the position which

God assigned to man in marriage, coupled with the newborn man's ability to talk about love, make him God's man here on earth.

Let us turn the attention of our teaching in the church to the task of training our men to be God's men.

Use every opportunity, every method of study notes, books, videos and seminars to strengthen the role of Christian man in the home. It will not demean Christian wives: it will set them free to demonstrate the beauty of Christ in our society.

The open home

There is one more area where the change in a Christian man is demonstrated within the home setting. It is in the area of hospitality.

Before a man becomes a believer his possessions hold sway. It is what he has which matters more than what he is. At a party he is introduced by what he does and what he owns. Property is of vital importance to man's status and self worth. To be known as the man who lives in the large house on the corner with the red sports car outside means that he has really arrived. But it is not a property which he particularly wants to share. It is his stake in reality and his only desire is *to build bigger barns* (Luke 12:18).

Men become strangely defensive over their homes. Lawyers have earned a lot of money and tackled a lot of difficult cases concerning neighbours who have encroached on another man's land.

It has been a feature of many of the letters I have received from Christian wives who have uncommitted husbands that their husband has acted with increasing irrationality regarding the home. 'If I have Christian friends round they have to come after he has gone out and leave before he comes back,' said one young woman. 'He won't allow any Christians in the home at all,' said another. 'If my Christian friends are here when he comes in he just walks straight through to the kitchen to get himself a drink. He doesn't even speak to them', wrote an older and clearly distressed lady.

Man is trying to hold on to something. He doesn't want to be invaded. He is in rebellion against God and that separation has the effect of separating him from other people.

Hospitality in one anothers' homes is practised far more amongst Christians than amongst any other social group, or for that matter any other religious society. The office, a party in a secular venue, or the pub, is the meeting place for much of the secular world.

We may have some way to go before we are like the early believers who had *everything in common* (Acts 2:44).

But we are moving along the right lines again by integrating our homes with our faith. The early Christians used their homes:

They broke bread in their homes and ate together with glad and sincere hearts (Acts 2:46).

It was apparently this frequent use of homes for praise which attracted the attention of their neighbours. Growth was the result:

And the Lord added to their number daily those who were being saved (Acts 2:47).

The change in a man is quite dramatic when he begins to open his home because he sees it now as the Lord's home. I am not recommending praise meetings which keep the neighbours awake after midnight, but I do know of a number of neighbours on council estates who have come to know the Lord because the church moved in next door instead of being a large gloomy building down on the main road.

Have a party!

The gift of hospitality is the special ability that God gives to certain members of the body of Christ to provide open house and a warm welcome for others. I commend it warmly. It is one of the gifts that you can safely experiment with. So kill the fatted chocolate cake and have a party.

Here are some more Bible references to hospitality.

Offer hospitality to one another without grumbling. Each one should use whatever gift he has received to serve others, faithfully administering God's grace in its various forms (1 Peter 4:9-10).

Share with God's people who are in need. Practise hospitality (Romans 12:13).

Hebrews adds the lovely thought,

Do not forget to entertain strangers, for by so doing some people have entertained angels without knowing it (Hebrews 13:2).

I have noticed that hospitality-gifted people are usually happier when they have guests in the home than when they are on their own.

Nor are hospitality-gifted people worried if someone comes when the place is untidy. They simply tell you to clear a space and sit down. The visitor is never made to feel an intruder.

Whilst not every believer has the God-given gift of hospitality, there is no doubt that when a man becomes a follower of Jesus, the possessions of this world are seen in a different light because they are seen in the light of God and of eternity.

It is that kind of a change which the non-Christian notices, because it is so startling a miracle to see a man using his home instead of holding onto it. It is what we do with the things of this world which are heard long before our words are listened to at all. That is newborn man, restored in the home. Now what about newborn man and money?

Chapter 12

Renewed in attitude towards money

'Money makes the world go round, the world go round,' is an old song. Even older is the saying, 'Money is the root of all evil.'

That is a misquote from the apostle Paul who actually wrote,

For the love of money is a root of all kinds of evil. Some people, eager for money, have wandered from the faith and pierced themselves with many griefs (1 Timothy 6:10).

If you make money your main friend then you will surround yourself with financial problems. Whether the markets are going up or coming down you will have problems choosing what to buy or what to sell. If the house market is growing, you may want to trade up; if it is in recession, accompanied by high interest rates, then you have worries about holding on. All of it demands sharp decisions; you are truly pierced with many griefs.

Jesus made an even stronger comment when he indicated that money was often elevated higher than a friend, becoming a god to be worshipped.

Notice that it is Matthew the tax gatherer who records the statement,

You cannot serve both God and money (Matthew 6:24).

Matthew gathers this statement by Jesus into a section of teaching about storing up treasure in heaven. He is recording it as a word of advice and warning for the followers of the Master. Hate and love, devotion and despising are the contrasts given. Luke the historian, with his more careful eye for historical accuracy, puts the saying into a challenge to those who loved money. Luke records Jesus' teaching about a shrewd manager aware that he was soon to be made redundant who reduced outstanding bills to other customers so that those customers would help him out when he came to be in need. The same contrast between two masters, one who is loved and the other hated is again the key to the phrase,

You cannot serve both God and money (Luke 16:13).

Our western world has been built upon a desire to possess. Salesmen are taught to place the object being sold into the hands of the buyer in order to increase his desire. In the case of a motor car, the salesman places the buyer inside the object for a 'test drive'.

The little child sat in front of the television to keep it quiet soon learns to say 'I want' in response to the advertising.

Money produces the power to possess and just as all power corrupts, so money becomes the owner rather than the owned. Money becomes the god not the slave, the master rather than the servant.

One of the miracles of newborn man is that he begins to conquer that which has controlled all of his previous life on earth.

D L Moody, an American evangelist of a hundred years ago, is reputed to have said, 'No man is truly converted until his pocket book is converted.' In our modern day, a man's credit cards need to be under God's authority.

Guidelines

Newborn man has the benefit of clear instructions in the word of God concerning his use of money. They start with practical help on how to give at least a tenth of it away.

Every believer is under direction to give some of his finances to support and advance the Kingdom of God.

He is told to set aside thoughtfully a carefully decided, specific amount, and to do it with cheerfulness. The Greek word *hilaros* provides our English 'hilarity'. Newborn man is laughing all the way to the church.

Each man should give what he has decided in his heart to give, not reluctantly or under compulsion, for God loves a cheerful giver (2 Corinthians 9:7).

Paul goes on to say that the gift of giving actually stimulates thanksgiving to God amongst the recipients of the gift and returns in the blessing of prayers on your behalf; prayers which release the grace of God into the situation of the giver.

And in their prayers for you their hearts will go out to you because of the surpassing grace God has given you (2 Corinthians 9:14).

Specific amounts given with cheerfulness seems to be the key to having control.

For the Jews, their giving started with their tithes and was supplemented by their offerings and special gifts.

The tithe was a setting aside of a specific amount, usually accepted to be one-tenth.

I do not believe that tithing is an optional extra for Christian believers.

The new-born man must lead the way in realistic giving. He must be taught why and how. The Holy Spirit will guide him as to who he should send his gifts to, in addition to supporting and expanding the work of the local church fellowship. Giving to the work of God is one of the first signs of a change of life-style which will be noticed by other, unconverted men.

They will see the reality of faith in the realistic terms of the use of money.

The effect of tithing

Money has such a hold upon modern man that he is startled when newborn man is set free from its domination. Secular man is challenged in his worship of the god of money when newborn man uses his money to significantly worship Jesus.

Tithing seems a good place to begin. Your personal circumstances will influence whether the tenth is calculated on gross pay (before deduction of income tax, national health payments and pension fund contribution) or on take home pay. The principle is that the first tenth is set aside for God, not what is left over when all the other bills have been paid.

Everyone that I have talked to, speaks of how the nine-tenths now seems to go further than the ten tenths used to go. In practical terms the setting aside of the first tenth into a separate charity account or wallet makes us look carefully at all our expenditure. It is a time when unnecessary and wasteful purchases are discarded. We take a new look at what we are worshipping. The end result is money over at the end of the month when at the beginning of the month we set the first tenth of our income apart for the work of God.

Tithing was started by Abraham, known as 'Abram' in his younger years.

He had been in a lot of trouble. Lot, his nephew, had chosen the plains of Jordan for himself and his family. He settled near what looked like very pleasant cities called Sodom and Gomorrah.

It was a time of constant skirmishes between the kings of local cities. An alliance of four kings came into the area to deal with a rebellion by the kings of Sodom and Gomorrah.

Why, after twelve years of paying taxes to the stronger kings, Sodom and Gomorrah chose to rebel in the thirteenth year is not made clear.

It was a mistake. They were wiped out and because Lot was in the area, he and all his family and goods were taken away into captivity and slavery.

Abraham could not allow the defeat to stand. He was eventually going to rule the whole area; with his nephew captured, he had to act or else he would have been open to blackmail.

He did so by calling on his crack personal bodyguard. Exactly three hundred and eighteen trained troops. They pursued the jubilant, and quite likely drunken conquering army, routed them and recovered Lot and all the goods belonging to Sodom.

On his return Abram is met by Melchizedek, king of Salem (Jerusalem). Melchizedek had not been involved in the fighting; maybe because his city was a neutral state or perhaps because Jerusalem was too good a stronghold to be attacked by any other kings.

In an amazing preview of the New Testament, Melchizedek brings out bread and wine to Abram.

King Melchizedek is described as priest of God most high. Abram recognises the need to set aside money for the work of God and in thanksgiving gives a tenth of everything to Melchizedek.

In return, Abram is blessed first by the servant of God on earth:

Blessed be Abram by God Most High, Creator of heaven and earth. And blessed be God Most High who delivered your enemies into your hand (Genesis 14:19).

Then, soon after, by the word of God from heaven:

Do not be afraid, Abram. I am your shield, your very great reward (Genesis 15:1).

Clearly Abraham was not going to be the poorer for setting aside a tenth of all that he had for the work of God.

If Abraham started the practice, it was God who confirmed it through Moses.

The commandments were given to Moses on Mount Sinai and applied from that moment on to all the people of God. Leviticus sets out the regulation clearly enough:

A tithe of everything from the land, whether grain from the soil or fruit from the trees, belongs to the Lord; it is holy to the Lord. If a man redeems any of his tithe, he must add a fifth of the value to it. The entire tithe of the herd and flock — every tenth animal that passes under the shepherd's rod — will be holy to the Lord (Leviticus 27:30–32).

So apparently if any of the grain or fruit from the tithe was used for home consumption you added an extra 2 per cent to the tithe money, and made it up to 12 per cent.

Tithe for rejoicing

Deuteronomy chapter fourteen contains further guidance
on the subject of tithing. The Levites, the priestly servants
of the Lord, were to be cared for out of the tithes. But there
is also the intriguing suggestion that some of the tithe can
be used for rejoicing. The people of God are not hardened
by their level of giving. Some is used to revere the name
of the Lord, some is used for the family to eat in the presence
of the Lord with rejoicing.

Newborn man can be extravagant in his giving, secure
in the knowledge that God wants his people to rejoice. If
Abram began the practice and God confirmed it through
Moses, then all the prophets commended it and clarified
it and underlined the principle of tithing.

One of the often quoted passages is,

*Will a man rob God? Yet you rob me. But you ask, 'How do
we rob you?' 'In tithes and offerings. You are under a curse
– the whole nation of you – because you are robbing me.
Bring the whole tithe into the storehouse, that there may be
food in my house. Test me in this', says the Lord Almighty,
'and see if I will not throw open the floodgates of heaven and
pour out so much blessing that you will not have room
enough for it. I will prevent pests from devouring your crops,
and the vines in your fields will not cast their fruit,' says the
Lord Almighty. 'Then all the nations will call you blessed,
for yours will be a delightful land,' says the Lord Almighty*
(Malachi 3:8-12).

I quote at length because Malachi the prophet, as messenger
of the Lord, touches on the three basic principles of tithing.
First, it is not an optional extra; it is a command which the
Lord expects to see fulfilled. Second, your attitude to money

is seen by God and by the nations round about to be a clear indication of how highly you value and how realistically you worship the Lord. Third, the blessing of God's love which follows obedience to his command is also intended as a witness to those who are not yet members of the Kingdom. So maybe this shows in your clothes lasting longer, or your car running better.

The floodgates of heaven swing on the hinges of God's love for the world. He wants the world to see and know about His goodness. I believe that tithes and offerings are a part of God's plan for his people of every age. Jesus never cancelled the instructions regarding tithing:

Don't think that I have come to abolish the Law or the Prophets; I have not come to abolish them but to fulfil them (Matthew 5:17).

In what way does Jesus fulfil the instructions concerning tithing, other than by the practice being continued in the church of which He is the head? There is evidence that the first disciples clearly understood this. Jesus indicates a blessing for those who give. There does seem to be a spiritual law in regard to sowing and reaping:

Give and it will be given to you. A good measure, pressed down, shaken together and running over, will be poured into your lap. For with the measure you use, it will be measured to you (Luke 6:38).

Remember this: whoever sows sparingly will also reap sparingly, and whoever sows generously will also reap generously (2 Corinthians 9:6).

Newborn man is to be marked out by his giving to the work of God.

Most churches are failing to grasp the opportunities for growth which are present at the moment because of a lack of staff members. At the same time, people who have trained in our Bible colleges are unable to find spheres of ministry. The handicap is always caused by lack of money. Newborn man needs to be taught, from spiritual birth, that his commitment to Christ is to be clearly shown by financial transactions as well as songs of fellowship.

Why hold back?

Why the church has been afraid to declare this is probably due to the Devil's lie that church is only after your money.

The church does not expect anything from an unbeliever, but it must teach the believers to set aside their tithe for the Lord.

Where the church has been scripturally bold in its teaching of tithing, that has been a factor in rapid conversion growth.

In South Korea it is estimated that about one in three of the nation are Christian believers. We would be satisfied with that; they are praying that it will be two out of three who are believers by the end of the century. Asked to analyse their growth, their leaders named prayer as a key. They do not hold conventions for music and praise, they hold them for prayer. They go to their mountain retreat centres, not to listen to Bible teachers but to engage in prayer. Prayer meetings start the day, every day, with prayer. On a Sunday, the first gathering is for prayer. Members search the Scriptures for the promises of God which are to be fulfilled that day and then claim the fulfilment of those promises.

The second key was seen to be fasting. There are just not enough hours in the day to fit in as much prayer as is needed. The only answer was to use eating time as praying time. No one starved to death and miracles of answered prayer began to be seen.

The third key factor to growth was the one which surprised me most. They named tithing as essential. The first believers tithed their income to fund the small work of their churches. New converts were taught the blessings of tithing. The extra funds paid for extra publicity, extra gospels for distribution, extra pastors, teachers and evangelists. This in turn resulted in still more converts who were taught to tithe and released the funds for a city wide programme of evangelism. In turn the next wave of converts released the funds for an area wide campaign and then the money to build new buildings and so on into yet more growth. If we are seriously going to reach the United Kingdom for Christ then we must see a return to biblical teaching on tithing.

Newborn man's first witness to his unconverted friends will be over the new value he places on his money: he can give it away with joyfulness.

A special gift

All believers are to give to the work of God's Kingdom. Some believers will then be discovered to have been given the God-given gift of giving. The gift of giving is the special ability that God gives to certain members of the Body of Christ to contribute their material resources to the work of the Lord generously and cheerfully.

Paul indicates that one of the advantages of the gifts of staying single is that you have more money available to give away, probably because you don't have a mortgage to pay.

I would like you to be free from concern. An unmarried man is concerned about the Lord's affairs – how he can please the

Lord. But a married man is concerned about the affairs of this world (1 Corinthians, 7:32-33).

The person with the God given gift of giving does not ask the question, 'How much of my money do I give to God's work?' but rather asks, 'How little of God's money do I keep for personal needs?'

By the way, you don't have to have large amounts of money in order to give generously. Jesus' comment about the widow at the Temple shows that fact (see Mark 12:41-44).

I have often felt that the gift of giving has not had a chance to develop in most of the churches of the United Kingdom because we have not even started at the level of giving tithes and offerings. In no other area will newborn man make a more significant contribution than in the area of giving.

Opportunities for evangelistic outreach and witness will abound as newborn man sets aside his tithe.

You want to reach the missing men? Then teach the men that you have got how to tithe for the Lord.

Chapter 13

Reclaimed in society

Recent years in the United Kingdom have seen the emergence of what has generally been called 'the renewal movement'.

There has been a strong emphasis upon the work of the Holy Spirit within the believer and through the church. Books have been written about signs and wonders, and many sermons have been preached on the theme of 'restoring the Kingdom'.

The renewal movement has attracted a lot of media attention both for and against, and the man in the street has often been made aware of this new breed of Christian who puts his hands in the air to sing and even jumps about a bit.

Jesus certainly spoke about the Kingdom of God here on earth:

Jesus went throughout Galilee, teaching in their synagogues, preaching the good news of the Kingdom, and healing every disease and sickness among the people (Matthew 4:23).

The Kingdom, then, was associated with movement and teaching and healing.

To one of the teachers of the law who answers his question 'wisely', Jesus says,

You are not far from the Kingdom of God (Mark 12:34).

So it is possible to be a member of the Kingdom of God somewhere here on earth: *The kingdom of God is within you,* said Jesus (Luke 17:21).

So we have both a mystical and private aspect to the Kingdom of God and we also have a manifest and practical outworking of the Kingdom.

The Kingdom is built by faith in men's hearts and it is also worked out in lives and fellowships and communities.

The place of social action

It has been heartening to see the evangelical wing of many traditional denominations, having been influenced by the renewal movement, taking an active interest in social affairs.

It has always been the work of the church to build the Kingdom; not by an overthrow of existing political powers but by a considered and creative renewal of society within the framework of law and order. To ask the church to stay out of politics is asking for the impossible. Political decisions affect society and it is within society that the Kingdom is being built. The church cannot leave politics off its agenda because politics are on God's agenda.

Recently, therefore, Christians have begun again to make their voices heard in places of power and outside on the streets of our towns and cities. They always used to do this and it is only the last generation which had failed to do so.

Paul puts it quite succinctly when he says,

*For the kingdom of God is not a matter of talk but of power
(1 Corinthians 4:20).*

Christians within the renewal movement have been
learning again that battles are often fought by prayer in
heavenly places and that these battles can be won in the
Lord's name.

Once authorities of darkness have been moved away then
there are new opportunities on the ground to build and
extend the Kingdom.

Let me suggest some of the areas in which the newborn
man will make the mark of God's Kingdom upon modern
society.

He will do so in the areas of law and order. Recent years
have provided ever increasing statistics of crime. In most
areas small robberies are no longer investigated by the police
because the chances of tracing the stolen television and
getting evidence that will stand up in a court of law are so
remote that it is not worth police time.

Even more disturbing is the growing attitude in some
sections of society that if the goods are owned by 'them'
(the state, the authorities, the bosses) then we can take those
goods – as long as we can get away with it.

So shops and stores, workplaces and offices are
plundered of millions of pounds' worth of goods in a single
year. Not only does this have an effect on the economy
and on prices; it also has a serious effect upon the
consciences of those who steal. The Kingdom principles
are quite clear.

*He who has been stealing must steal no longer, but must
work, doing something useful with his own hands, that he
may have something to share with those in need (Ephesians
4:28).*

Paul states that he is talking about the Kingdom and the life-style of the reclaimed man.

Be made new in the attitude of your minds and put on the new self, created to be like God in true righteousness and holiness (Ephesians 4:23-24).

So the newborn man lives a new way. The stealing which stops may have been the stealing of a bit of time or small quantities of paper from an employer who knew nothing about the theft. But giving up stealing does something for the man who stops, and begins to build the Kingdom of God.

Pay it back!

In some cases the stolen goods are larger in quantity. It has always been a feature of Christian revival movements that restoration of past debts has taken place, and has made an impact upon the unbeliever.

For example, in about 1908 when the men from the Welsh revival came to the town of Keswick for a Bible convention, the local post office ran out of postal orders as Christians repaid debts of years' standing to people all over the world.

Then there is the lovely story linked with the preaching of the Irish evangelist, Willie Nicholson, in Belfast. A time of revival had broken out and men were being converted every day. Many of them worked in the Belfast shipyards. As they entered the Kingdom of God with power so they realised that equipment that they had previously stolen from their workplace had to be returned. The flood of goods taken back was so great that the yard had to close for a long weekend whilst the items were all entered back into stock and put away in the stores.

Is it possible to offer everyone a chance to *work, doing something useful with his own hands (Ephesians 4:28)* in an age when everyone agrees that unemployment has come to stay? Few economic commentators doubt that the unemployed statistics are one of the weapons which are used to keep inflation under control.

It seems to me that this very area of unemployment opens up a practical way for Christians to demonstrate the distinctiveness of the Kingdom.

Newborn man, reclaimed in society, has a code of honesty. He also has a balanced attitude toward authority. Again the Scriptures are his guide:

Everyone must submit himself to the governing authorities, for there is no authority except that which God has established. The authorities that exist have been established by God. Consequently, he who rebels against the authority is rebelling against what God has instituted, and those who do so will bring judgement on themselves. For rulers hold no terror for those who do right, but for those who do wrong. Do you want to be free from fear of the one in authority? Then do what is right and he will commend you. For he is God's servant to do you good (Romans 13:1-4).

We must note that Paul was writing in far from democratic times. He does not seem to be merely being tactful in case his letter was read by government officials in Rome. He appears to be stating that newborn man builds the Kingdom of God within the existing structures of society.

What if the structure itself is corrupt? There did come a time when laws were passed which sought to force everyone to worship Caesar as Lord. The Christian believers refused to compromise on that issue but in all other areas they acted as exemplary citizens paying their taxes when due even if those taxes were used to station occupying forces in their own homeland.

Peter reinforces the same teaching,

Submit yourselves for the Lord's sake to every authority instituted among men: whether to the king, as the supreme authority, or to governors who are sent by him to punish those who do wrong and to commend those who do right. For it is God's will that by doing good you should silence the ignorant talk of foolish men. Live as free men but do not use your freedom as a cover up for evil; live as servants of God. Show proper respect to everyone: Love the brotherhood of believers, fear God, honour the King (1 Peter 2:13-17).

Peter goes on to show that our submission is even to unjust and harsh rulers, and Christ is our example of commendable suffering.

Prayer support

What an impact could be made in our society if a whole new generation of newborn men began to back the powers of government even when they, themselves, had voted for the party which failed to gain power.

Paul gives us directions along these lines:

I urge, then, first of all, that requests, prayers, intercession and thanksgiving be made for everyone — for kings and all those in authority, that we may live peaceful and quiet lives in all godliness and holiness (1 Timothy 2:1-2).

Paul stacks up all the words that are linked to prayer. He speaks of approaching our Lord and begging Him to answer our prayers on behalf of those who are in authority. We are so confident of answered prayer that we are ready with our thanksgiving.

In a disturbed and sometimes destabilised society, with its multiracial mix and multi faith make-up, we may soon find that it is the constant commitment of newborn man which becomes the cement holding together the structures of constitutional government. To any who want a revival of true patriotism it is the Christian faith which offers a way of hope.

Praying for those in authority inevitably leads to involvement. Intelligent support requires both interest and information and it is not long before something needs to be done which you are equipped to do on your own. Most traditional denominations have steadily lost members over recent decades. Industry compensates for a dwindling work force by more up-to-date machinery, work study and productivity agreements.

Strangely, many churches have tried to continue with their Victorian programme of events and, often, in the constraints of their Victorian buildings.

Keeping a structure from the past, especially one which is labour intensive, has prevented Christians from playing their full part in modern society.

Nowadays there are so many church events and meetings demanding our attention that we have no time to fulfil our role in society as salt and light. Newborn man must be set free from too much church routine so that he can become a guardian of good within society itself.

Reclaimed man has the ability to care for that which is good, and under the leadership of God he can become a wise leader within a community or area. Our world is confused by all the claims for individual rights and no one is balancing that with the need for collective responsibility.

Two essential areas in desperate need of Kingdom

guidance are the areas of schools and broadcasting. The powers of local parent/governors groups have increased as schools have begun to handle their own spending and set their own budgets. One headmaster said to me that he would need the wisdom of Solomon. For newborn man this is not a problem. It is exactly the wisdom from above which he can expect to receive as he prays. That man should be a member of the local school governors board. If you haven't got a strong Christian presence in your local schools then you ought to search out the suitable candidates within the fellowship and encourage them to stand for office.

Your encouragement will include an immediate reduction of their church work load in order to give them enough time to carry out their new duties.

Opportunities in broadcasting

Then with new facilities increasing the activities of local radio stations there is again a gap in the market for creative people to handle religious affairs on radio.

No one is offering a platform from which to conduct airborne evangelistic crusades, but sane, hard working and exciting people are needed to get involved in religious broadcasting on local radio. Sometimes a local item goes on to collect national interest and you would be the one who brought it to people's attention.

It is significant to note that when there is a revolution in a country, the tanks are immediately sent in to take control of the radio station.

Whoever influences our schools and our broadcasting will affect society in the future.

These are the places where reclaimed man should be deeply involved. The church's fear seems to be that such areas of work will take people away. One minister who got involved in local broadcasting is now a full time religious affairs producer. Does that mean that he has lost his call to ministry? Not at all. He is exercising a ministry in a different sphere. What must not be allowed to happen is that he becomes isolated by the church itself. He needs more support in his new ministry than he has ever had before.

The Christian man and conservation

Not all that long ago, if you asked a man in a street interview to tell you about the ozone layer he would have probably looked totally blank. Now there can hardly be anyone who hasn't heard about the hole in the ozone layer and many people will even be able to tell you that it is the fluorinated carbon gases which have caused the problem – although I doubt if they could give the chemical formula.

People in the United Kingdom are, at the moment, not very troubled by the idea of the earth warming up. Winter temperatures that out perform those of Benidorm, Spain, are welcomed and the thought of staying at home for holidays and eating real English fish and chips has its attractions for many.

There has been widespread public anger however at the destruction of wild life and its habitat. Nature programmes are a highly rated feature of every television channel. Share prices have been affected as ordinary people have made it known that they don't want their pension fund money invested in companies which are recklessly polluting the environment.

So the new brand of green orientated consumer has been developed. Industry and commerce have led the way but even the politicians have jumped on the bandwagon, eager to please and ready to show their green credentials.

Burning rain forests and civil wars which prevent crops

from being planted are both pollutants on a global scale.

Christians have often been at the forefront of efforts to help homeless and starving refugees. Christians have usually supported the freedom of individuals, even small Amazon tribes, against the vested might of governments and gold-miners.

We are now entering an era where the media coverage of green issues will be increasingly relegated to columns of news under small headlines on inside pages.

Not all that long ago, the crisis was so new that it filled the front pages.

Media interest in the environment may well be declining. This is exactly the time when conservation needs to be undertaken on a larger scale than anyone ever realised in order to preserve planet earth.

If mankind is to avoid disaster early in the next century, we need more than cosmetic adjustments, we need cosmic action. The man to lead the drive to save the world must be newborn man. Who better to help put things right on Planet Earth than those who are in touch with Earth's maker? Recreation and restoration need to be carried out by those who are in sympathy with the role and purpose of our world. Here again, Christ's/Man is the leader of the pack.

When profits are involved then manufacturers are quick to relabel their products. When additives and E numbers were in the headlines some companies listed the long name for a colour source in order to give the impression that there was no 'added' colour.

In the green market a few companies have launched old brands under new titles to give the impression that these are now environmentally friendly. In a few cases new product lines are launched so quickly that long-term research has not even been carried out at all.

I have been disturbed by the number of recalls in both

manufactured goods and foodstuffs which indicate, at the very least, a production line inadequately staffed or inspected or, at worst, a failure to test products on a long enough time-scale for fear that another manufacturer will get into the market first. Christ's/Man may not have the chemistry expertise to check out every product but he does have an inbuilt warning system and a hot line to heaven itself. The Holy Spirit promises to lead us into all truth and He is quite capable of doing what He has said that He will do.

The real areas which need to be changed require a change of will. What if all the Christ's/Men in our land were to check out all the products that they use and get rid of any that are contributing to the destruction of our world.

Some items would have to be replaced by more expensive products: it would be seen that we really meant business if we were prepared to pay the extra price. Some replacements would also involve us in extra work like the tin of polish replacing the spray can. It would be seen that our concern is real not illusory. Why not start on the spray cans today? Newborn man must lead the way in redeeming the time and in recreating the world. How about our use of water? What about conservation of electricity?

Opportunities for witness

All of this involvement in society from the social strata of the workplace via school to the supermarket is bound to produce opportunities to restate the faith which Christians hold.

It will not be without areas of conflict especially when powerful self interest groups are involved. Our source of strength comes from God and He will enable our faith to stand firm.

All of life will become an outreach to other men. It is men who must lead the way to a new society. We need more recruits for the battles that lie ahead. In the 1960s destructive forces were at work, and some of their seeds of darkness have only just borne their awful fruit. The 1990s demand a new generation of newborn men. By some people's standards they will be labelled as 'fanatics'. A friend of mine defines a fanatic in this way: 'A religious fanatic is someone who loves a religious system more than I do. A Christian fanatic is someone who loves Jesus Christ more than I do.'

Too often in the past we have only been seen as religious fanatics, and that is bad. We have been addicted to our meetings and our timings and to our special buildings. No wonder people have turned away. But if we were to become the magnet which points men to Jesus Christ then we would see the fulfilment of the promise that, He, Jesus, *will draw all men to myself (John 12:32).*

Jesus spoke of the lifting up as being a work of salvation for society, just as the people of Moses' day were saved from destruction in the desert. Mankind is rapidly making a desert out of planet earth. It is time that salvation came.

On our own we cannot even get a hearing for our message of hope. Clearly we must learn to stand together and walk together and work together. And that means fellowship within the Church.

Chapter 14

Redeemed in the Church

An Anglican minister friend of mine has recently completed a series of teaching sermons on the great words of the Bible – 'faith', 'forgiveness', 'fellowship' and so on. He then took the courageous step, or made the mistake, whichever way you look at it, of setting his congregation an exam to see just how much they had learnt from the series. Of course he didn't call it an exam, or they would never have done it; he called it a 'survey'. They were given two weeks to fill the papers in at home and return them anonymously into a collection box in the church entrance.

My friend is now in need of rest and recuperation. He felt that he had been crystal clear in his teaching but was amazed to find that most people had not heard or had totally misunderstood him. You will remember the preacher's slogan,

I know you believe you understand what you think I said, but I am not sure you realise that what you heard is not what I meant.

It was the answers to the question on the subject of 'fellowship' which interested me. Some were coloured by the traditional view that the building was the church, not the people. Most defined fellowship as the cup of tea and a biscuit at the end of certain events.

Koinonia (fellowship) was used in secular Greek writings for the closeness of a man and a woman in marriage. It was almost interchangeable with intercourse. That is the word which the New Testament picks up to describe the closeness which is meant to exist between believers.

Promises in the plural

Many Christians miss the fact that the majority of God's promises made in the New Testament are promises made in the plural, to the whole group, not only to the individual. In other words they are not for individual selfish aggrandisement, they are for collective shared blessing:

Peace I leave with you, my peace I give you (John 14:27).

It is a promise to the fellowship, to the group; the individual experiences the peace *within* the protection of the group of believers.

When Paul states the same truth, *the peace of God which transcends all understanding, will guard your hearts and your minds in Christ Jesus (Philippians 4:7)*, he also states it in the plural form. The promise is to the group, to the fellowship of believers. The individual appropriates the blessing within the fellowship.

Now there *is* an aspect of salvation which is quite clearly personal and individualistic.

If anyone hears my voice (Revelation 3:20).

If anyone is thirsty, let him come to me and drink (John 7:37).

I am the living bread that came down from heaven. If anyone eats of this bread, he will live for ever (John 6:51).

Every man must have personal faith and place his personal trust in Jesus Christ for full and eternal salvation. The early confessional statement of the church was probably to say 'Jesus Christ is Lord'. In those four words we summarise so much of eternity. Jesus Christ is Lord of salvation, Jesus Christ is Lord of eternity. Jesus Christ is my Lord. You cannot be saved by other faith than your own. Others though, will have played a part in leading you towards the place of faith. Others will have prayed for you and talked to you and taken you along to events to hear about faith. You didn't discover it all on your own without the fellowship of believers. The church does not do the saving, but it provides the environment within which people can find personal salvation.

Having made that discovery and having received the eternal forgiveness of God then salvation in the New Testament takes on a distinctively corporate aspect. Newborn man is part of fellowship.

Promise after promise is stated in group terms:

He who began a good work in you will carry it on to completion until the day of Christ Jesus (Philippians 1:6).

The promise is made to the whole church, the whole group, the complete fellowship gathered in the garrison town of Philippi:

My God will meet all your needs according to his glorious riches in Christ Jesus (Philippians 4:19).

What a marvellous promise of heavenly supplied earthly

resources, promised to the group, to the fellowship. The supply is not given to the individual to squander on personal needs, it is for the group to use in mutual blessing. Newborn man is part of a fellowship, God's team, the together people of God.

There is one body and one spirit (Ephesians 4:4).

Caring for one another

Within that intimacy newborn man learns to be involved in 'one another' ministries. The group are to learn to care for one another. It is surprising how, in so many church circles, there is little caring ministry for each other.

Much of our lack of balance and failure of strength in our churches has been due to our failure to teach just how much we really do belong together. We have also failed to follow the Bible instructions to look after one another:

Love the brotherhood of believers (1 Peter 2:17).

That is a theme which is repeated many times in the New Testament. Paul's advice is,

Be devoted to one another in brotherly love. Honour one another above yourselves (Romans (12:10).

Each of you should look not only to your own interests but also to the interests of others (Philippians, 2:4).

Therefore, as we have opportunity, let us do good to all people, especially to those who belong to the family of believers (Galatians 6:10).

We seem to have lost this biblical note of special treatment for our fellow believers. It has been overshadowed by Victorian values of individualistic attainment or replaced by modern government practice of putting everything out to competitive tender. The result has been that people discern no value in belonging to the church. I have even met people who felt that although they were saved they were under no obligation to belong to any church or indeed to belong anywhere at all.

The biblical principle for newborn man seems to lie in a new emphasis upon preferential treatment for those who are within the fellowship of believers. Are some of the shops and companies near to you owned by believers? They deserve your constant support. Your trade will enable them to install new equipment or increase their stock and prosper still more.

Fellowship must be seen in terms of advantageous trading positions or it remains empty rhetoric rather than realistic brotherhood. I have met men who perceived of more material advantage to their business if they joined the masons or the Conservative club than by belonging to the church.

Newborn man moves from being a self serving individual to being a servant of the people of God. In this he is serving his Lord and following in the footsteps of the Master:

Just as the Son of Man did not come to be served but to serve and to give his life as a ransom for many (Matthew 20:28).

Didn't Jesus do everything for all men? Clearly not. The parables are one indication of his two levels of teaching. The parable was proclaimed to the whole crowd. The deeper explanatory teaching was then given to those who stayed on as disciples willing to learn more. You could argue that even the ransom for sin which Jesus paid is only efficacious for those who believe: it is therefore a blessing from which the believer alone benefits.

Benefits of fellowship

The benefits to the believer of belonging to the fellowship of God's people have begun to emerge in recent years within some of the charismatic groupings. They are anxious to demonstrate that they are building an actual Kingdom of God here on earth and their members have been encouraged to act along those lines. I have heard of neighbours getting converted because they learnt of the 'love offering' given to a Christian who has just lost his job and is unlikely to find new employment.

The non-Christian is not after material gain in joining the church, but he has to be convinced that there is such a thing as the love of God poured out into men's hearts.

Newborn man belongs to the fellowship. He is redeemed within it. Within that loving fellowship, he finds a time for inspiration and uplift.

There is clearly a trend in modern society and the Church would be foolish to ignore it. It is a trend towards people participation. The Church must be one of the very few places where a one-man show is still performed. In the arts world only a very talented actor would attempt to do a one-hour programme on his own.

As I travel around the United Kingdom I am noticing that more and more Christian groups are moving towards using the Sunday morning period for a time of worship which expresses joy and confidence. Increasingly, worship times are getting longer than the hallowed hour. It is not primarily the time for deep theological teaching; it is the opportunity for uplifting participation in the things of God. That does not imply a neglect of the Word of God in such meetings.

New Christians are looking for the inspirational word that will be relevant to the challenge, conflict and opportunities for the coming week. We all need the encouragement that comes from such ministry. This is how we are built up and grow in our faith.

There is no reason why the morning should not move into a meal together so that fellowship can be furthered over food.

Children should be welcomed in these meetings as long as they are not disruptive. The sooner the child experiences the moving of God upon His people the sooner those children will become equipped for the work of God and move in the things of God themselves. Certainly by Senior school age, all the children of believers ought to join the whole church in its worship time. There is no reason why the gifts of the Spirit should not be exercised by the children's faith.

These Sunday morning praise times are not primarily evangelistic opportunites although people do, sometimes, get converted. The friends and family of new Christians come along because they are impressed by the changes they see in newborn man's lifestyle. The realisation that 'church was never like this' has an attraction to those who are ready to think again about Christian faith. The next specific evangelistic event will certainly be working on prepared ground.

The participation level in the times of praise should be intentionally high. Many people should participate, probably limiting their 'sharing' to two or three minutes. In the early days people need to be invited and prompted, encouraged and trained to take part so that people learn that it is allowable to take part.

Those on the platform with the responsibility for leadership must give a clear lead. If you want people to be free to put their hands in the air, then the leaders must be seen to confirm that by doing it themselves. In a larger meeting where amplification is needed in order for people to hear, then those who wish to take part may well have to refer to a leader during a music time before taking part to bring publicly the individual contribution which they feel that God is giving through them.

With smaller groups. I suggest that you limit the contributions made by any individual to no more than three. In other words, they may introduce a song from the floor, or read a scripture, or bring a special word, all as short contributions, but not take over the whole meeting.

The truth must be taught that Christ's/Man is part of the building of God and each one has a part to play in building the Kingdom.

Leaders do not need to be afraid that other gifted people might emerge from the rank and file. God-given gifts do not threaten the God-appointed leaders. Restricting new abilities prevents growth whereas encouraging it could lead to a larger church or even to the planting of new churches.

It is especially within the worship that the areas of man's mind which were in a state of discord are brought into the harmony of joy.

Man, who is so often negative in his outlook, is opened to the positive healing work of the Spirit of God.

Let us not give up meeting together, as some are in the habit of doing, but let us encourage one another (Hebrews 10:25).

That verse must never be used as justification to move more and more Christian activities from their rightful place in the home to church premises. When Christ's/Man is functioning within his home as priest and leader then a number of indispensable midweek activities at church become redundant. Newborn man moves on in discipleship. As he does, so he becomes a more disciplined man. He moves from being an unreliable husband and parent to one who can be relied upon to play his part in the home and in the bringing up of a family. Nothing is more important and nothing more neglected than the art of good parenting.

No two children are alike, even within the same family, but there is no reason why future generations of parents should make the same mistakes as previous generations. It is within the fellowship of the Church that parents can learn the art of parenting.

Thankfully a new wave of teaching is available dealing with Christian principles applied to the reality of twentieth-century western civilisation. The principle gives the foundation for actual practical help.

Much of this teaching is demonstrably of more benefit when it is given in small group situations. A group of eight or ten can learn to trust each other and can all participate in real discussion. The opportunity provided by such small groups allows more leaders to be trained and can provide the first outlet for a gift of Christian teaching to be exercised and recognised. Modern man is usually restless in mind and spirit because he has been unable to find his rightful place in the sphere of home and family. Christ's/Man can lead the way to the place of rest concerning subjects which have been areas of conflict.

As Christ's/Man learns to control his aggression within the home he learns also how to handle conflict in his place of work. He becomes the peacemaker to whom others increasingly turn for assistance. Jesus did say:

Blessed are the peacemakers for they will be called sons of God (Matthew 5:9).

Jesus, the Son of God, made peace for man through the shedding of His own blood.

Christ's/Man acts in the role of reconciler and peacemaker by allowing the Lord's presence to flow through himself into the lives of others in need of peace and harmony.

Christ's/Man discovers that his protective shell of hardness is being put off like an old garment and is replaced by the strength of kindness.

Be kind and compassionate to one another, forgiving each other, just as in Christ God forgave you (Ephesians 4:32).

That kindness is an outworking of the goodness from within. Newborn man can afford to give away kindness because he is no longer threatened by an inner emptiness. He used to have to hold on to his anger over injustice, real or supposed; it helped fill his life. So much hurt is caused by lack of forgiveness and usually the hurt is caused most of all to the one who cannot forgive. Christ's/Man inherits from his new faith the God-given ability to forgive. He is therefore powerfully able to get rid of areas of conflict which would have seriously damaged his mind, and in turn, his physical well-being.

Such new attitudes do not turn newborn man into a weak man; far from it. The non-Christians are the first to recognise that such miraculous qualities are new strengths.

It does not mean that there will be no righteous anger over injustice and exploitation within the world. Nor does it imply that Christ's/Man will accept the status quo that he finds within the church.

Christ's/Man, like his Lord, will be a man of action. He will certainly expect the church to become more gift-orientated rather than role dominated. Much of church life has been parcelled out for the past forty years as jobs that needed to be done in the church, rather than looking for the gifts that God has given to His poeple and using those gifts to the full.

No one has seriously challenged the jobs or questioned the validity of wasting manpower on some of them. All we have done is to go on filling the positions inherited from the past, with only minor modifications to the programme.

The only serious change that I have noticed over the years since the last war has ben the introduction of the job of 'elder' to a number of the free church denominations.

In times of emergency, undertaking a role for which we are not gifted can be acceptable. If a fire breaks out and I know where the fire extinguihser is kept, I will tackle the blaze until the real firemen arrive. I may or may not manage to contain things a little. But as soon as the gifted fire-fighers arrive on the scene, I hand the whole task over to them.

The New Testament clearly teaches that God gives gifts to his people so that they can do the work of the Kingdom.

Christ's/Man is aware that he has been given spiritual gifts as a result of the grace of God which has entered his life. The Greek word CHARIS for grace, and the word CHARISMA, for gift, are clearly closely related. Spiritual gifts are 'grace-gifts'. Spiritual gifts are the overflow of God's grace.

Christ's/Man also knows that his gifts have not been given to him for his own personal glorification. They are only of value when he uses them to bless all the other members of his fellowship. Peter sums it up clearly and beautifully,

Each one should use whatever gift (CHARISMA) he has received to serve others, faithfully administering God's grace (CHARIS) in its various forms (1 Peter 4:10).

Chapter 15

The Example
The Man above all men

Who is this Jesus anyway? He lived so long ago; why should we bother with Jesus today? We don't remember much about the birth of Nero of Rome, somewhere around the same time in history; why remember the birth of Jesus at Bethlehem?

Who is this Jesus? He never wrote a book himself and yet more books have been written about Him than about any other person in history.

Who is this Jesus? He never led an army and yet His teaching has conquered and changed more nations than any other great general so that in our world today one billion 796 million identify themselves as His followers, that is one in every three people who are alive. World wide, over 63,000 more people have become Christians this week, naming Jesus as Son of God and as their living Lord.

Who is this Jesus? He never had worldly wealth to establish a powerful political organisation and yet His power is still felt in modern society. Jesus has a relevance, a reality and a recognition in our day that is unmatched.

No one else compares to Him. No other leader, no president of a nation, is so vitally alive as Jesus. No one else is changing modern day men in such a radical way.

Jesus takes hold of lives and transforms them. He gives men a new dynamic for life a new dimension in life and a new direction to life.

Jesus gives men a victory over evil and a power to live right which man has not known since the days of the garden of Eden. Jesus takes depressed men and gives them joy and hope. He takes scared men and sends them out as strong men singing about their salvation. He gives bewildered men a sense of purpose and makes sense of the crazy world that we live in.

I have seen so many miracles in the lives of men that I would need the space of the *Encyclopaedia Britannica* to list them all.

Who then is this Jesus, who can so change lives two thousand years after his own death? Was He just a man or was He the unique, the special and only Son of God? I became a Christian, or as I now prefer to say, I became Christ's/Man after examining the evidence. Let me present some of it to you. If Jesus is all that He claimed to be, then He demands our allegiance and our commitment. If He is only a good teacher, a religious leader and a Galilean guru then we can choose to ignore Him and live life any way that we please.

If, when you have looked at the evidence, He is shown to be the unique Son of God and the only Saviour of all those who believe, then we had better believe.

It may be unwise to ignore a great teacher but it is eternal suicide to ignore God.

Read the story

Let's take a look at just one of the records of the life of Jesus, the record written by Mark, probably written at the prompting of the big fisherman, Peter.

What did other people think about Jesus? What did Jesus believe about Himself? Let's start with some of the religious people of Jesus' day – the Pharisees.

The Pharisees were a group of very religious men. They saw Jesus as a danger to their religious traditions:

Then the Pharisees went out and began to plot with the Herodians how they might kill Jesus (Mark 3:6).

In their religious zeal, the Pharisees aimed to keep the ten commandments. To help them do this they had worked out a very elaborate list of things which could be done in daily life and of things which would make life impure and unclean.

They had a whole catalogue of 'Don't do this and don't do that'. Their traditions were important to them. They had 365 rules, one for every day of the year, and 264 regulations, detailed plans of conduct.

Jesus came along and disturbed these people. Real religion, Jesus argued, real contact with God didn't come through any outward ceremony, however keenly you try to keep the rules. You can only come into contact with God, said Jesus, when your heart is pure.

The Pharisees scored highly at outward ceremony: one hundred and eighty at every throw. But they all knew that in their hearts they were failures; their thought life, the motives that other men didn't see because they were hidden inside the mind. These motives and thoughts were far from good enough to meet God's requirements of purity.

Jesus offered a salvation which changes men from the inside but the Pharisees didn't want to know. They just wanted Jesus out of the way because He threatened their settled system.

Jesus still threatens the settled systems of many religious

people today. Are you a church-goer or are you a Christ's/Man? Have you been keeping God in His place, in a little section of your life but under your control? A bit of church-going now and again, when it fits in with other plans?

Jesus will not have it that way. He demands to be Lord of your time. He wants all sections of life under His control.

The Pharisees knew that Jesus did not fit into their religious system.

The family

At the same time His own family were convinced that He was mad and so they came to take Him away to save further embarrassment:

When his family heard about this, they went to take charge of him, for they said, 'He is out of his mind' (Mark 3:21).

At the time, Jesus was healing crowds of suffering people. Was that madness? Just before, He had given sight to the blind, straightened out the life of someone who had been bent double for years and given work to men who were unemployed. Is that madness?

Maybe it was madness by this world's selfish standards. The world says, 'What is mine I keep', or, 'What is another's I'll get.' Jesus just gave and gave. It was God's extravagant abundance. But was it madness? The conclusion that I have come to is that Jesus was the most completely sane man of all time.

The teaching of Jesus

Jesus taught about the wonder and majesty of the

Creator/God. He spoke of God's love and God's desire to save, finishing that section of His teaching by reminding men that to reject such love would lead to eternal judgement. That was logic, not madness.

The teaching of Jesus has been acclaimed throughout the world because it sets out the highest duty of men. Jesus wasn't mad.

I am so glad that the early Christian records tell us that after the death and resurrection of Jesus, Mary His earthly mother, James, His stepbrother and the other stepbrothers joined the Christians and worshipped Jesus. They thought that He was mad at first but they came to realise that He was God. Then they became His disciples.

The teachers of the law in Jesus' day said that Jesus was evil:

And the teachers of the law who came down from Jerusalem said, 'He is possessed by Beelzebub! By the prince of demons he is driving out demons (Mark 3:22).

The 'law' referred to was the Jewish religious law. These men, the lawyers of their day, spent a lot of time writing down in technical jargon the various religious debates of their day.

They then spent the rest of their time explaining that technical jargon to the ordinary man in the street — for a small fee, of course.

They were the teachers of the law because of their logical approach to everything. They observed that Jesus clearly had power over evil forces. That meant either that Jesus was God and that is why He had such power, or that Jesus was a man who was in league with evil and that was why He had control.

They didn't like the idea of Jesus being God because then

the logical thing would have been to worship Him. So they settled for Jesus being in league with evil.

In league with the Devil?

Jesus, quite correctly, points out that this is illogical. He says,

How can Satan drive out Satan? If a kingdom is divided against itself, that kingdom cannot stand. And if Satan opposes himself and is divided, he cannot stand, his end has come (Mark 3:23-26).

The powers of evil don't let powers of evil destroy them. Internal civil war wouldn't do the Devil any good at all. Jesus logically inferred that if He was able to cast out the powers of evil then that proved that He was stronger than such powers.

Jesus was stronger than the Devil, so it follows that Jesus was far more than just a mortal man.

What about the powers of darkness? They themselves said that Jesus was the Son of God:

Whenever the evil spirits saw him, they fell down before him and cried out, 'You are the Son of God' (Mark 3:11).

They screamed it out because darkness is always afraid of light: 'You are the Son of God'. And Jesus agreed.

When the Pharisees said that He was a danger to their religious traditions Jesus said that their formal religion was worthless.

When friends and family said that He was mad, Jesus said that those who did the will of God would realise otherwise.

When the teachers of the law said that He was in league with the powers of evil Jesus pointed out that such a thing was impossible.

But when the powers of darkness, the evil spirits, said that He was God, Jesus agreed and then gave them strict orders to go away and keep quiet. His plan was to make Himself known through His disciples. The choosing of the twelve apostles follows immediately. Jesus wouldn't let the evil spirits talk about Him but He did send out His disciples to preach about Him. Those disciples went out to declare that Jesus was the Son of God.

Who is this Jesus? He is the Son of God.

He came into our world of darkness to bring light to those who would follow Him. He died on a cross to bring about the salvation of all who believe. He rose triumphant from the grave to demonstrate His supremacy over all things.

All the four gospels recording the life and teaching of Jesus Christ have one striking thing in common. They all place their major emphasis upon the final week in the life of Jesus on earth.

In my Bible, the four gospels take up 144 pages of print. Nine pages cover the first 30 years of Jesus' life. Eighty seven pages cover the three years of Jesus' ministry; His sayings, His parables, His teaching and His miracles. Then 48 pages concentrate on the final few days; from Jesus triumphant entry into Jerusalem to His death and resurrection.

One-third of all the gospels are written about one week, out of more than 1,700 weeks that Jesus spent on earth.

There is no doubt that the emphasis is on Jesus' death for our sins and His resurrection for our full salvation. Christianity is not about church buildings or church ceremonies. It is all about Jesus Christ.

The living Saviour

Christianity is not about doing good when convenient and supporting the church when it needs a new roof. Christianity is all about the once dead, but now living Lord Jesus, living as Saviour; our Saviour, on the inside of our lives.

Mark's gospel is typical of the stress on Jesus' death and resurrection. Jesus often used the special Bible title, 'Son of Man' in reference to Himself:

The Son of Man is going to be betrayed into the hands of men. They will kill him, and after three days he will rise (Mark 8:31).

They were on their way up to Jerusalem, with Jesus leading the way . . . Again he took the Twelve aside and told them what was going to happen to him. 'We are going up to Jerusalem,' he said, 'and the Son of Man will be betrayed by the chief priests and teachers of the law. They will condemn him to death and will hand him over to the Gentiles, who will mock him and spit on him, flog him and kill him. Three days later he will rise' (Mark 10:32-34).

Jesus set out to Jerusalem knowing that, at the end of the road, there was a cross. That means that Jesus set out to die before His ministry was even half over. In fact, Jesus set out on His journey to the cross even before time began, because He knew that only His death could open up the gates of heaven to those who would believe.

Jesus set out to be our Saviour. Isn't it time that we set out to be His modern day followers, the Christ/Men of today? If He deliberately chose to die for us, then shouldn't we choose to live for Him now?

The only reasonable and realistic response we can make to the amazing activity of God is the response of wholehearted commitment. That means handing over control to Jesus. Jesus doesn't want a corner of a man's life, He wants control. It is not just a bit of decency that is required but, rather, dedicated discipleship.

There is no entry fee for a man to pay to join real Christianity. Jesus has paid all the price; but your annual subscription is all that you are, placed under His daily control.

When Jesus arrived in Jerusalem He was betrayed to the Jewish religious authorities by a man who had seemingly been a follower and disciple for three years. Judas Iscariot had heard Jesus' teaching, seen Jesus' miracles and lived in the company of Jesus' other disciples. If ever there was a warning for religious people, Judas Iscariot is that warning.

It is obviously possible to be religious and yet not be right with God. Outwardly, you can be in the crowd of followers of Jesus. At the same time, inwardly, you can still be completely self centred, money motivated and proud of your religious associations.

Attending church is not enough. Having your name on a church roll is not enough. Baptism is not enough. You must, personally, turn from sin and trust fully in Christ. You not only have to be in the crowd with Christ; Christ has to be in you. Are you Christ's/Man?

Pride the barrier

The most common factor that hinders men from becoming real Christians is our pride. We want to do it for ourselves. We want to get our own lives right by our own efforts, so that God has to accept us. Men need to accept the fact that only God's salvation can reach and restore the parts that our failure and sin have destroyed.

A man has the power, of course, to say 'No!' to God. God gave each one of us a personality, an inner will, a central decision-making ability. He won't override your choice. He reaches the doorstep of your life but won't force His way inside. Only you can invite Him into your life.

A man can say 'No!' to God, but if he does, he is lost and nothing can save him. The Bible says:

Salvation is found in no one else, for there is no other name under heaven given to men by which we must be saved (Acts 4:12).

There is no other name. No other religion leads to God.

Give him the name Jesus, because he will save his people from their sins (Matthew 1:21).

'Jesus' was the Greek form of the name Joshua, meaning, 'the Lord saves'. There is no other name and there is no other Saviour. I'm not saying that other religions do not contain any wise teaching, but they do not have any eternal salvation.

No one else can save you, only Jesus. He said so Himself,

I am the way, and the truth and the life, no one comes to the Father except through me (John 14:6).

No other religion leads to God. There is no other way. *I am the gate*, said Jesus. *Whoever enters through me will be saved (John 10:9).*

Through him (Jesus) we have access to the Father (Ephesians 2:18).

There are those who suggest that it doesn't really matter what you believe just as long as you believe in something. That is nonsense. It does really matter. To those who say that all religions eventually lead to God, we have to answer that God Himself does not agree. There is no other name – only Jesus.

The emphasis of the Bible is on the death of Jesus for our salvation. His death was awful, hideous, monstrous, vicious. He was laughed at, spat upon and beaten with the scourge whip that cut a man's back wide open. The sky itself went dark. Jesus' head rolled from side to side. The crowd mocked Him, wagging their heads and chanting like a football crowd, 'He cannot save himself'.

Failure or triumph?

They were right, of course. He could not because He would not. He couldn't save Himself, because He was dying to save you and me. He couldn't look up to heaven because He was taking our hell, bearing our banishment. He encountered the separation from God that we deserve; so that we might be saved from eternal separation.

He himself bore our sins in his body on the tree (1 Peter 2:24).

His death wasn't a mistake. God doesn't make mistakes. The death of Jesus was essential for our salvation. It was in our place. No other name can save us. No other way can bring us back to God.

If you want to be right with God, you must believe in the power of Jesus' name and walk in His way.

Take another look at Jesus. Here is the man above all men. He is magnificent. He is worthy of the total dedication of your life.

Are you Christ's/Man? What is involved in being Christ's/Man? For Him it involved a cross. For me it involves a discovery and a commitment; a discovery of truth using my mind and a commitment of life using my will.

Jesus is the truth. Jesus' way is the way. I am here on earth, in order to know God in heaven, so that I can live for Him in eternity. I discover the truth.

Then I commit my inner will; that part of me which makes the crucial decisions decides to make Jesus Christ my leader, my example and my Lord. His way is the way forward for my life.

Look what He has done. He has done something for me that I could not do for myself. The only realistic way to say thank you is to hand over the control of life's destiny to this amazing Jesus.

He remakes me into a man by the power of God the Holy Spirit, and then as a Christ's/Man I help to remake this world. In His name I begin to turn the chaos back into God's kind of order.

What do you now have to do to get in on the action? First you must face up to the fact of failure. Your life hasn't been all that it should have been. It hasn't even been all that it could have been. There has been too much darkness. Now Jesus is calling you into His light. Accept the new beginning and the forgiveness that is offered. You cannot come to God just when you like. You can only come when God calls you, and God is calling you now. So make it real today, once and for all.

Here are the words of a prayer which has helped hundreds of men to take this crucial step of faith. If you pray the prayer, write and tell me so that I can send you some more material which will help you to be a Christ's/Man in our modern world.

Action Page

This prayer could change your life.

No one else can pray these words for you. It has to be your sincere, personal response to God. It will help to make it very much more real if you pray aloud.

O God, you know all about my life. Forgive me for trying to hide from you. I admit my failure. I have sinned against you and hurt other people by my words and thoughts and actions. I need your forgiveness. I haven't even tried to give you the first place in my life. Thank you for still loving me.

Lord Jesus, thank you for dying on the cross. I believe that your death has made the forgiveness of my sin possible. Please God, forgive me, for Jesus' sake.

Holy Spirit, I need your power now, to give me the assurance that my sins are forgiven and to give me the strength to turn away from the things I know to be wrong. Come into my life and take control. Help me from this day to live for the glory of God, one day at a time.

O God, hear my prayer.

Amen.

The wonderful thing is that God does hear our prayers. He has heard your prayer.

My prayer for you is that you will now have a growing inner assurance that your life has been made right with God, through Jesus Christ.

My prayer for you is that you will experience the real presence of God the Holy Spirit in your life.

My prayer for you is that God will use your life to bring others into His glorious Kingdom.

Postscript

A final word about promises

These words are especially for those wives who have found faith but whose husbands do not, as yet, share their personal faith in Jesus.

You must never lose hope.

Why are you downcast, O my soul?
Put your hope in God, for I will yet praise him, my Saviour
and my God (Psalm 42:5).

Do not let your heart envy sinners, but always be zealous for
the fear of the Lord. There is surely a future hope for you,
and your hope will not be cut off (Proverbs 23:17-18).

Those who hope in the Lord will renew their strength. They
will soar on wings like eagles, they will run and not grow
weary, they will walk and not be faint (Isaiah 40:31).

'For I know the plans I have for you,' declares the Lord,
'plans to prosper you and not to harm you, plans to give you
a hope and a future' (Jeremiah 29:11).

Be joyful in hope, patient in affliction, faithful in prayer
(Romans 12:12).

May the God of hope fill you with all joy and peace as you trust in him, so that you may overflow with hope by the power of the Holy Spirit (Romans 15:13).

Love always trusts, always hopes, always perseveres (1 Corinthians 13:7).

You will receive the gift of the Holy Spirit. The promise is for you and your children and for all who are far off — for all whom the Lord our God will call (Acts 2:38-39).

Remember to keep hope alive.